In the Age of Artificial Intelligence

Choosing Purpose Before Code

DR. ELIZABETH M. ADAMS

Learn more about the author at www.eadams.tech

ISBN: 979-8-9949497-1-9

Publisher: Dr. Elizabeth M. Adams

Publisher Consultant

Table of Contents

A Letter to the Reader

You're holding a traveling copy.

This book was released to move through human hands.

If it serves you, keep it as long as you need.

When you're ready, pass it to someone who needs it next.

One request, if you feel led:

Leave a single sentence about what this book helped you name.

Then let it travel on.

If you'd like to keep it and purchase additional copies to place into circulation for others, please do so.

—Dr. Elizabeth M. Adams

Preface

Sometimes in life, we find ourselves chasing momentum, always moving fast, staying busy, or trying to keep up with what's trending. We pursue titles, chase opportunities, and reach for the next shiny tool, especially when it comes to artificial intelligence. Everyone's building something. For a while, it feels like we're on track, doing exactly what we're supposed to do.

But speed doesn't always mean we are headed in the right direction.

For some of us, somewhere along the way, we start to feel something. A feeling of disconnect between what we are chasing and what we believe. That's when things begin to shift. The shift is not always dramatic. It can be quiet. We stop asking "What's the latest and greatest?" and start asking "What's the impact?"

We start to notice the difference between automation and accountability, and what tech can do and what it ought to serve. We choose differently. And for some of us, including me, that shift leads to choosing purpose before code.

In the Age of Artificial Intelligence: Choosing Purpose Before Code is a lyrical memoir, a reimagining of leadership as a practice of presence through purpose. It's a walk in life.

This memoir sings with notes of frustration, confusion, love and joy. It sings in fragments and footsteps. It weaves memory with meaning, and story with a quest to help us understand how we might discover our unique leadership purpose. Some parts linger with questions, thoughtfulness and care. Other parts land with conviction.

This book invites readers first to become available to their most authentic selves, honoring both their gifts and limitations. Accepting this invitation may reveal a leader's true purpose, making them available to influence the worlds they inhabit in an unlimited number of positive ways. In ways that are no longer in conflict with who they are.

In a world that rewards urgency and performance, this book centers on emotional integrity, wisdom, and the regenerative power of one's defined self. It proposes that leadership discovery begins with love: unguarded, unbound, and without expectation. When we meet ourselves with compassion, we become purposeful leaders who guide others with clarity, generosity, and grace.

This book is for today's moment.

Because in the Age of AI, our most significant advantage isn't speed. It's knowing where our internal compass is pointed, so when the wind picks up, we are ready to move.

Move with purpose.

PART I
THE STIRRING

No Mother's Child

"The wound is the place where the Light enters you."
— Rumi

I was six years old when my mother passed.

My world didn't pause for empathy or sympathy. I was expected to keep moving. And I did. Living in a male household with a family who loved me dearly, but not gently. I remember going back to elementary school the day after my mother's funeral. No therapy, right back into class. A little girl, six years old, trying to make sense of the gaping hole in her world.

I was unable to describe the incredible loss of my mother. My teachers and the school staff were very loving during this time, and I felt their warm energy. I didn't know how to name it or place it. I had not yet developed a heart to hold that energy, the same indescribable, beautiful energy I received from them throughout the school day. Their energy was available whenever I was around them, but it wasn't the dominant energy I felt most of the time as a little girl. I didn't know how to place it. Yet I learned early to recognize the difference in energy.

When not in school, I experienced a different kind of energy. Six brothers. A father. A grandfather. My permanent familial figures at home influenced everything. Their love was real, but it was masculine, structured, protective, and often raw. Vulnerability was never modeled in my home. I grew up being tough because that's what survival looked like in our house. My tears were often private. With my brothers, competition was our love language, and so, in public, I was strong.

We competed for attention, for space, for pride. We competed because it was a way to say, *I'm here. I matter.* I became a great athlete not just because I was exceptionally gifted, but because it gave me a way to feel love, or what I thought was love. Winning became my gift to my family. It became my way of being seen. Success was easy for me. Resourcefulness was my birthright. But over time, my achievements became like a drug. They numbed the ache I couldn't name, the absence of my mother's presence and, in her absence, a different kind of energy. The kind I felt in elementary school, delicate, safe, kind, beautiful, and incredible. Yet I had no permanent connection to that energy. The kind of love energy I felt before her untimely death was gone. Removed. Silenced.

And that absence was the beginning of a painful road of discovery. A desire to find my place among loving energy. Somewhere. Again.

Yes.

There were many women around, wonderful aunties, cousins, and neighbors. My father remarried. But still, I was no mother's child. I didn't have a soft place to land, that daily reminder that I was loved just for being. I longed for years for what I believed was the healthy development of love, the kind that teaches you how to receive without earning, how to cry without shame, how to show up without needing to prove your worth.

Without it, I grew up strong. Capable. Respected. But not vulnerable. Not tender. Not available to myself, and so unable to truly be available to others in the way my being needed.

My developmental years taught me how to lead through grit. But they didn't teach me how to lead with compassion and understanding.

I felt it at my mother's viewing. Too young to comprehend, I thought she was sleeping and couldn't understand why so many people were crying. I remember comforting a family member, rubbing their back as if to say, *I'm sorry.* That was my first time feeling my heart sense what someone else was feeling. A young empath was forming, perhaps. It's my first recollection of how LOVE shows up for me, by having a heart for others. That moment might very well be the first sign of how I was born to live.

I was too young even to imagine that hard lessons lay ahead. Lessons to teach me how to find my own way to love. Lessons of compassion and patience would come later, through loss, through longing, through the quiet invitation to become available to myself. Available to myself to learn myself. To learn how I'm made, where life wanted me to go, and how life wanted me to lead.

This is where *In the Age of Artificial Intelligence: Choosing Purpose Before Code* begins. Not in my accolades, but in the tension, in the ache. It starts with accepting my truth, reconciling that I was no mother's child, and that my desire to see others happy, thriving, and free was my way to BE in this big old world.

For years, I felt like God was being extra cruel and unkind by throwing me to the wolves of life. Tired of so much pain and loss, I became desperate. And so, for 30 years, I've been on a journey to learn how to tap into my own source of love and find ways to sustain it. I wanted to offer it to others freely.

I am still learning.

I am still learning how to accept love and what it means to me. I'm learning what it means to be available to myself and others. What purpose means. Where I thrive and when I feel depleted. The clues have BEEN all around me for years. Yet there was nothing external I felt was helping me with the how, how to deal with my yearning. Just a constant push to climb the corporate ladder, with the understanding that any joy would need to exist outside of work and not in leadership, or else I would be perceived as weak and unserious. Something that feels eerily familiar to this day.

I don't recall one person asking me as a child, "How do you feel?"

I've Always Known

"To choose joy in a world that doesn't yet know your name is to remember your worth aloud."
— Dr. Elizabeth M. Adams

I was twenty when I asked my best friend if she was happy.

It wasn't a question we were used to. We were used to shopping, singing, dining, gossiping, and laughing until our stomachs hurt. We chose lightness. We were both introverts, and it felt good to be around someone who understood the beauty of silence. But underneath it all, something began to stir in me, something that couldn't be soothed by brunch or living room dance parties.

She was shocked when I asked her, "Are you happy?" It seemed to come out of nowhere. But for me, wanting to ask the question had been building. Each time we traded stories of difficult times, I noticed something: we spiraled. As we shared more stories in our trusted space, the deeper we spiraled. We became a container for each other's trauma. I didn't know how to vocalize, *I don't want this.* It had never been modeled for me. I'd always seen friends and sisters share pain as a form of trusted connection. But I didn't want to take on her trauma and discomfort. I didn't want to carry it. And yet, I needed the comfort myself. I succumbed often due to the need to share my own pain, and she didn't mind carrying my weight. In hindsight, I see how that part of our friendship led to unhealthy future relationships with others.

Still, something deeper in me was trying to be. A new way of living, a new way of relating.

That question, "Are you happy?" was layered. It wasn't just about curiosity. It was a doorway. I wanted my dear friend to reframe her story and speak more positively about her life. But I didn't have the tools to guide her in that direction. I didn't know how to articulate what I meant. So "Are you happy?" became my way of setting the stage. If she said no, I could say, "Well, let's get you happy." If she said yes, my wild passion for joy would leap forward.

Even then, I knew what fed me. Even then, I knew what I was designed to be available for, to whom, and to what.

I could listen for hours to someone sharing their joy, their dreams, their hopes. Listening to someone express their glory made me feel alive. Even now, when I look at the books in my digital library, books I've purchased over the last thirty years, eighty percent are self-help and self-discovery. Clearly, I was looking for answers or trying to find myself in them. I didn't know I had a source I could tap into to let me know if I was on or off track. I didn't have a well of wisdom nearby. Maybe that's part of why cocooning felt better. It gave me space to search inward, to listen for something deeper.

What I know about myself today is this: I prefer to share uplifting news. I know I can spiral into depression if I focus too long on what's going wrong. I've found mechanisms to help. I enjoy practicing boundaries and the comfort of rituals. All of this has shaped my current experience. It has shaped my leadership love journey, which now guides how I live.

I desire to lead from a place that considers joy as sacred. Now, when I ask myself, "Are you happy?" it's not a fleeting check-in. It's my spiritual invitation. It's about refusing to be a container for trauma when I was born to be a vessel for light.

I've always known.

Even when I didn't have the words, even when I didn't have the training, even when I was twenty, I was asking questions that startled people. I've always known that love, joy, and generosity were my native language of inspiration, especially when given the space for authenticity.

I am here to affirm, to uplift, to support within my spiritual boundaries. I've learned to speak more about what happiness means.

Naming the Tensions

I woke up one morning, a year after graduating with my doctorate in Leadership of Responsible Artificial Intelligence. I needed to accept the truth. I had danced around this truth for years. Every Artificial Intelligence leadership book inside me, every framework, every keynote, every brilliant idea would never feel satisfactory until I dealt with the tension inside.

The tension was soul deep.

It was the tension between who I believed I was supposed to be, based on my external accomplishments, and the part of me that could no longer hide. The truest part was ready to lead.

People would say to me all the time, "You need to monetize AI." And if the space were safe enough, I'd respond, *I don't know how.* But that wasn't the real issue. The real challenge for me was that I was never drawn to monetization. Clearly, my library of self-help books validates this way of being.

I've always been drawn to a person's lived experience. To see how they were doing, how they were making sense of the world. How they found happiness not by describing it to me, but by my listening to their word choices, their tone, and by observing their physical and facial expressions. I've been drawn to what they were carrying.

I felt forced into an ecosystem of transactions when all I wanted was to understand the human first.

When I was younger, I was constantly told I was "nosey," a way of describing how I was always in someone else's business.

I knew I loved stories. I loved listening to my dad tell us stories of his childhood.

I loved studying how people interacted with life and technology during my doctoral studies. When I chose qualitative research, it wasn't just a preference. It was a full-body yes. It was me. I loved everything about it. The nuance. Analyzing stories, coding data, creating themes, and discovering patterns. For me, it was more than an art. It was the sacred act of listening, a sacred act of honoring. Placing stories and lived experiences on a pedestal to be respected.

So here I was, speaking and teaching all over the world. And after each event, each effort, each initiative, I would feel a personal dip. For years, I thought, *Maybe I'm not good on panels. Maybe I'm not good at keynotes. Maybe I'm not good at writing.* But deep down, I felt empty and unfulfilled.

I also didn't think that my return to Minnesota, after things didn't work out in D.C., Richmond, and Savannah, was a calling. I thought it was bad luck knocking at my door once again, as a cruel trick led by God.

But a year after returning from Savannah, I had a moment of clarity. The tension I was feeling needed to be addressed at home in Minnesota. And that was a rude awakening. It saddened me. I knew I couldn't control this part of my personal journey. I was to face the yearning to do life differently right here at home.

Living frustrated, I was at the point of giving up again. I thought, *I'll find a job at a local store and just fall out of the light.* I considered night shifts as an overnight stocker. I was tired of trying. I wanted peace.

It was around this season in life that I picked up Parker Palmer's book, *Let Your Life Speak*, for the fifth time. As I opened it, I said, "God, this is it. I'm going to read this because it's here, but I'm tired."

As I began to read, something felt different. I wasn't just reading in hopes that something would leap off the pages and give me a complete understanding. I was no longer hoping.

I was reckoning.

I needed to sort this out. I needed to name it. Because if I didn't, it would keep showing up. And I'd keep isolating.

Here, once again, was an invitation. An invitation to get naked to thyself. Drop the identity that the world knew of me and ask God yet again, "What do you want from me?"

I didn't mind isolation. Isolation was familiar. It was comfortable. I enjoy being by myself. But this wasn't a call to suddenly become extroverted. It was a call to address the tension I'd felt for a very long time, and more specifically, the ten years I've felt since working in AI.

I had built my life of loss around something external to make it digestible and acceptable to me. Like not being invited to the table, even though I was clearly the most qualified to speak on a particular AI topic. Or the countless job rejections that chipped away at my confidence. I convinced myself I knew why.

"Oh, they keep giving me the stiff arm. They are not interested in me or my voice." Those stories felt true, and maybe they were. They made sense. They made me feel better. But things didn't get better. Not my finances. Not my soul.

Because this tension wasn't circumstantial. It was spiritual.

How do you resolve the tension of truly wanting nothing more than to know how people engage with life from a place of supreme interest and curiosity, while also being an award-winning AI influencer? How might I reconcile being someone on the world stage talking about AI trends, but really wanting to know what the neighbor two doors down thinks about AI?

My leadership in the world was taking me further and further away from my love of stories. That's the rub. I wasn't getting enough of that deep thing met. And so the tension kept pulling and pulling. Until, once again, I was working on things just to pay the bills.

I finally said to myself and to God, "You know, I don't have anywhere else to go. There is nothing 'out there' in the world that is calling me forward as deeply as what is calling me inward."

I was offering a nice smile to people I met and a framework to a client. I was on autopilot. But something happened.

Two truths emerged.

First, I really enjoy meeting people and learning about their way of life. That realization lit a fire in me. A beautiful, hopeful fire. The kind that says, *This is real. This is yours. Do more of this. Do it as often as you can, in large numbers. Feed this need. It's real. It's you. Don't be ashamed or afraid. Just start asking the questions you really want to know when you meet people. Just do it. It doesn't matter what the original meeting was for. Just do it.*

That was a terrifying feeling to acknowledge. But it was a beautiful knowing because in this truth, I find comfort. My body lights up. My spirit gets giddy. I'm full of anticipation every time I think my next meeting could be just like this.

During breakfast with a colleague, she told me I was sounding different, kind of like a preacher or evangelist. I certainly have felt that alignment from a worldly definition, but I call it something else. Leading generously with love. Giving this part of myself away for free. The part that wants to engage on an "are you happy" level to get to the stories.

This brings me to the second awareness.

I needed to connect more deeply with an elder community on a level away from my accolades. I needed their wisdom. I needed their guidance in the form of questions. I required less transactional interaction and more legacy connections. I desired a way to connect to those who have seen some things. Those who have lived through some things. Elders who have perhaps named their own tensions, explored them, and addressed them. I needed love, and I hoped to absorb some of it through wisdom.

So here we are. I accepted my truth. Something in me wants to enjoy people, gather them, talk to them, and be generous with my gifts.

When these feelings began to surface, I didn't know what that looked like. But I knew this. The words Artificial Intelligence were not in any of the things my BEING was asking of me. I was discovering what *In the Age of Artificial Intelligence: Choosing Purpose Before Code* was beginning to mean.

I experienced a spiritual invitation to check in with my highest self while spending time in Umeå, Sweden, as a visiting scholar. It was the first time in my life that I said yes to whatever wanted to be revealed, in whatever timeline. I would document it, write it down, note it, and send myself voice notes. I would be the phenomenon to study qualitatively. I would analyze patterns from my lived experience and see where they led. I gave myself a personal research question: "How does Elizabeth reach maximum internal happiness when removing worldly expectations?"

Naming the tension and developing a question was the first step toward living the truth. And my truth is leadership through love. My truth is people. My truth is generosity. And now, I'm finally letting that truth speak.

The Fire That Keeps Returning

*"Don't ask what the world needs. Ask what
makes you come alive, and go do it."*
— Howard Thurman

A familiar tension showed up once when scheduling a meeting to talk about AI. I really wanted to center joy. Joy is the first thing I think about before a meeting. Joy gets me excited even though I know the meeting will be about key performance indicators (KPIs), strategy, or frameworks. To help, I often use a blend of language, such as stewarding AI and aligning an AI strategy with the organization's core values. That is what makes the conversation acceptable to me.

But where I really get going in my meetings is when people share their work-life approach. When they openly and honestly share their optimism, their fears, hopes, and expectations. Ah, that is where my gift of generosity through listening and love shows up without ever saying that part out loud.

I am interested in how my client's leadership is shaped by culture, their lived experience, and their desire for more or less employee engagement. Whatever direction we choose, I know my team and I can deliver. That is where I excel. I've spent so long denying my true way of leading, with love and joy, that the rest of my skills now run on autopilot. They are sharp, absolutely, but they are not my whole story.

My work comes alive when I can connect personally with my clients. Learning about people's lives, families, travels, hopes, dreams, and fears inspires me. Transactional interactions leave me feeling disconnected. Genuine connections energize me. They offer a beautiful, hopeful fire, the kind that says, *This is real.*

But now I have questions. Not about whether it's true. I've always known it is, but I've never quite understood what it means to finally center love, generosity, and courage to be transformational in transactional spaces. What does that look like for me? How should I earn a living? How do I take my expertise and make it work for me?

Once, a colleague said to me, "Well, we can't all be Oprah and manifest clients by feeling our way into business." I was attempting to share my desire to lead in a way that felt more aligned. Her words stung more than she knew, and she wasn't being intentional. It stung because I had not been seen, and I wondered if I would continue to suffer leading differently than the way my soul was calling me to.

Since my early leadership days, I've felt this desire. But I didn't have systems around me to support it. It wasn't seen as a dominant vocation. It didn't come with a title, a salary, or a blueprint. For years, my desire to know people more deeply was pushed back, not suppressed, just quietly set aside behind the things that looked more successful.

Naming it now places it up front.

And if I were to dream a bit, here is what it might look like:

- Learning about people, their ways, their dreams, their hopes
- Stewarding resources to help them get where they are meant to go
- Giving generously, instinctively, without needing to be asked

Just recently, I felt compelled to donate to someone working on a documentary. That is what I mean. I learn what you want, and then I support it, financially, emotionally, and strategically. I've perfected stewardship. It's second nature. But I've never seen this modeled as a way of life. My deep desire was pushed far to the back of how "life" works.

And now, nothing else is remotely satisfying. My soul keeps returning to meet me at this point.

I am finally ready to lean in and figure it out. But it's scary. I know from experience that the inward journey can take time, time I do not feel I've. I do not want to go through another poor phase. I know the cycle:

I take a job out of alignment just to work.
It stresses me.
I start drinking and isolating.
Then I get a breakthrough idea, like AI.
I become successful because I know that system.
But I am still ignoring the thing that wants to be front and center.

This time, I am choosing differently. I am honoring the fire. I am trusting that the desire to know people and to steward their dreams is not a hobby. It's a calling. And I want to believe that if I center it, the rest will follow.

Because the fire keeps returning.

PART II

THE COCOON

The Cocoon Was Never
Meant to Be Home

*"You do not just wake up and become the
butterfly—growth is a process."*
— Rupi Kaur

Cocooning didn't start with a longing for transformation. It wasn't like I could point to any time in life that said, "Let's go inside and come out differently." That wasn't how it was with me. It started with exhaustion. One letdown after another, one failed try after another. I kept getting up from the blows in life, trying and trying and trying. I watched others rise as they appeared to have found their right way: the right path, the right vocation, the right way to lead and have meaning. And I felt stuck. I'd reach a point that felt like great success, and then, after sitting with the achievement, I felt hollow.

The exhaustion I felt could not be fixed with sleep. Not at all. Something was settled deep in my being and in my bones, and it was trying to speak. So many times the world felt too sharp, too loud, too demanding. I didn't wrap myself in silk and whisper, "I'm ready to become." In fact, my experience was quite the opposite. I wrapped myself in fear, in worry, in retreat, in disgust, in helplessness, in loneliness, and in frustration.

It was easier to blame the world for my troubles than it was to face the ache inside. I tried to face the invisible ache many times.

And slowly, the cocoon became safe and familiar. A place to escape.

I convinced myself I liked being alone. I told myself I was protecting my peace. I often declined invitations to gatherings, birthday parties, trips, and other social events. I didn't feel like pretending I was enjoying being social. But I didn't know that pretending was what I was doing at the time. I'd convince myself, due to my age, that I needed more rest, but really, I was hiding. I had forgotten about times in my life when I was the life of the party. I lit up rooms. I made joy contagious. I felt completely whole. That feeling was short-lived, but at least it was something really, really wonderful that I could return to in my mind. Because at one point it was real.

But now, sharing my light felt risky, invisible, and exposed. It felt costly.

So I stayed wrapped.

I had to face my inner struggles. I had to name the ways I went inward to find comfort, because that was what cocooning really was: a return to the only safety I knew. Growing up in a house of men, I learned to be strong, not soft. I learned to survive, not surrender. And when life got heavy, I went back to that place. I wrapped myself in silence and called it peace.

But that was never the end of my story.

I wasn't meant to live wrapped up, away from life and vitality. I had to name it. I had to own my part in it.

And then, slowly, I began to move. I started going out intentionally, awkwardly, and vulnerably acknowledging my inner self, saying, "Hey, I'm not sure what I'm doing, but how do I lead first, AI second?"

I opened myself to feedback. All kinds. The kind that stung, the kind that soothed, the type that confused me. I feared I'd be seen as weak, as performative, as someone kissing the ring. But then God touched my heart and said, "Go out in love. Do that. That is your job. Give love generously. You already know how to do that. Let me take care of the rest."

And for me, "the rest" meant everything:

- Where I'd live
- How I'd earn
- How I'd relate to others
- How I'd trust again
- How I'd lead without needing to be seen

Cocooning taught me what I wasn't. But God's love reminded me who I am.

I am generous. I am available. I am rooted in love. And when I lead from that place, I don't need wings because I am the wind.

The Backpack Full of Bricks

"When we can tell our story with tenderness, we become the sanctuary we've been seeking."
— Dr. Elizabeth M. Adams

I've always known that my North Star was trying to guide me. I've known where I was supposed to be headed for a long time.

Being in service to others has filled me in ways I am only now able to describe. I used to love serving lunch to church and community members.

As a child, during the summers, my brothers and I would visit my Aunt Bernice in Sacramento, California. She modeled what it was like to be in service to others. Often, she would gather us up, and we would head to church with her during the week. She would help organize lunch for anyone who needed a good meal. I remember being at the end of the line, handing a plate full of turkey, gravy, green beans, bread, and salad, and saying,

"God Bless You." First, I was told to, and second, it gave me a sense of how kindness should be shown toward others. I didn't know if anyone was with or without food or a home. My aunt never described the people we served that way. She would say, "We are going to serve lunch to the community." Perhaps this is where I began to be acutely aware of language. Because she saw them as people we were feeding, she gave them agency and dignity. I then saw them as people we were feeding. I didn't attach any meaning to their experience beyond our presence together. I thank my aunt for unknowingly teaching me an important lesson.

While service has been a staple in my life, I've also learned to serve others without attaching labels because serving felt good.

Once, I volunteered to sing Christmas carols at an Assisted Living Center. I'll never forget that day. While I do not remember the year, I do remember it was a cold, snowy December day in Minnesota. I packed up my car with my sound system and a few karaoke CDs and headed toward the center. I promise you it was at least 20 degrees below zero. But my heart was warm for service. Upon arriving at the particular wing, I learned that I would be singing to residents living with dementia. That didn't stop me one bit. I was going to give a full concert. Just as I had dreamed of singing *O Holy Night* at the Kennedy Center, I visualized myself there with my immediate audience. The residents were gathered around, and off I went. For an hour straight, I sang with love from the heart. One resident sat the whole time with both hands over their ears. I wasn't the least bit offended. Another shouted out racial epithets during my performance, and I wasn't fazed. In that moment, my only job was to serve in love and let love go to work in whatever way it wanted to.

Love also led me to fly across the country to care for and clean the home of a friend recovering from surgery. I remember that time clearly. I was struggling to find work. My funds were low to zero. My current situation didn't matter because, even though she owned a home, had a great job, and had plenty of food and clothes, I was better off. I had my health and my strength. I offered what I had: to be of service. Do I like cleaning and cooking? That would be a hard-and-fast no, but I saw a need for love and stepped in.

I've always loved to help.

I've also always loved getting in my car and going as far as I could safely, or becoming a tourist in a city next to mine. Each time I returned to Minnesota, I would drive and drive, finding a new neighborhood. I wanted to see the changes, the new stores, and the fancy shops. My being longs to explore and touch new things.

Professionally, frontier leadership carried those same inquisitive qualities. When it came to AI, I wanted to know why it wasn't working for everyone. I wanted to help others thrive by using my gifts and talents.

I've lived through global experiences, opulent events, and frameworks designed to bridge research and practice.

I knew the direction. I had the credentials. I had the map.

But I wasn't living as my True Self outwardly. I was in the secret places that no one would see. I was retrofitting myself into the ideals of the world around me, trying to sell my brilliance the way I saw others do it.

What looked like a backpack filled with academic and industry insights was actually a bag full of bricks. Heavy bricks. Heavy with expectations, limitations, and misalignment. A departure from serving others in a way that felt most like who I've always believed I was to be.

One of those bricks was my Responsible AI framework.

It was rigorous, thoughtful, and deeply valuable. I developed it as part of my dissertation, and upon graduation, I began trying to offer it to organizations to increase employee and stakeholder engagement.

I knew it could deliver results. It was designed with both academic rigor and industry experience in mind. Having led large tech teams and systems, I knew it would work.

But I was leading with the framework as the solution, not the story.

Not the soul.

After contemplating why it wasn't driving business success, I broke it down into five frameworks designed to help an organization complete a framework journey in 90 days. Still nothing. No interest.

Then I simplified the frameworks into one-hour workshops, tabletop exercises, and anchoring questions.

Suddenly, it landed.

What was different? Simplifying it allowed me to touch people, including leaders and employees. Simplifying it gave me space to understand their needs, organizational culture, hopes, and fears around AI. This design wasn't based on industry standards; it was based on my way of leading and my way of serving. I realized again for the hundredth time that when I lead with my True Self, people respond.

In this honest assessment about my passion and desire for how I want to show up as a leader, others get what they need. More importantly, I get what I need.

Connection. Curiosity. Clarity. Joy.

Now I am better positioned to handle the implementation side professionally.

But the shift wasn't in the framework.

It was in me.

My father used to say, "You never let grass grow under your feet." It was his way of affirming my drive, my need for evolution, connection, new stories, and constant motion.

I've always been a seeker of meaning, of impact, of places where my gifts could take root.

But I've come to realize that what I was hoping to find in the world had been tucked away because I had allowed the world's expectations to be front and center in my life.

For a long time, I mistook movement for alignment.

While leading and serving, I've reached many summits. Some were breathtaking. Some celebrated. But at the top, I often felt like something was off. I found myself asking, "Is this summit mine?"

Back down the mountain I would go, searching for answers for discernment.

Learning is not a mistake. Learning is a lesson, and in the Age of AI, something was definitely rearranging in me.

Ten years ago, my work in AI felt manageable. But in the last five years, the pace of new AI tools in the marketplace has accelerated. The noise has grown louder. Almost too loud.

In the midst of it all, my true self decided it could no longer be silent.

It reminded me that I can always find my way home if I remove the backpack full of bricks.

I can find my way home if I let go of carrying bricks to build bridges and building bridges through connections.

Naming My Darkness:
Living Out Loud

There is a part of me that I've kept quiet for years. Several years. Not because I wasn't ready to share. I wanted to. But it wasn't time. I had not done the work to leave it, bury it, and release it.

Hurt. Frustrated. Excluded. Kept out of rooms. Harmed. Lied to. And the list goes on.

I know what it feels like to return with "nice nasty," that sharp, polished edge of me that can cut with a smile. I've felt absolutely satisfied in it. Because at the core, I despise entitlement and ignorance. I always have.

But what I've learned is that my definition of those two, entitlement and ignorance, became a scapegoat. It was a way to attach meaning to someone or something that was often far from the truth. It gave me comfort. It gave me a story. In the moment, I felt justified in using foul language to describe someone I despised.

I own this part of me.

I still work on it. I still catch myself in it. I still feel the pull to name the wound. But I know now that those definitions, those attached meanings, have kept me from being vulnerable. They have kept me from trusting that Love will show me the way to my personal leadership style and way.

You see, love doesn't always come dressed in fairness. It doesn't always arrive with apology or recognition. That is because love should start with us. Sometimes love just whispers, "Respond with leadership. Respond with kindness and grace. Respond with who you truly are."

And who I am is Love.

That doesn't mean I allow my boundaries to be abused. That doesn't mean I stay silent in the face of harm. What it does mean is that I ask myself better questions. I've begun to ask: Who am I when I lead from a place of clarity? When I am super clear about what I like, what I do not like, and how I want to show up? Who am I when I situate myself in a place of feeling whole?

I saw my first Fabergé egg in 2017 while living in Richmond, VA. The Virginia Museum of Fine Arts holds the largest collection of them. I've always wanted to see one, and when I did, I was in awe. They represent a symbol of luxury, and the craftsmanship is simply unmatched. They are rare. They represent legacy and timeless design.

When I allowed others to define my way of being in the Artificial Intelligence space, I sent a message to the universe: my value is negotiable. I signaled that I was willing to fragment myself to belong, to earn a seat at the table. I let external validation define my worth.

But leadership rooted in clarity and love calls for us to lead differently. For me, it calls me to treat my essence like a Fabergé egg—jeweled, precious, sacred. The value of the egg does not shift with the nature of the looker at a museum. No. It remains exquisite, untouched, and unfazed by the gaze.

This was and still is a pivotal lesson for me.

To understand that people may still carry entitlement. They may still act from ignorance. But my job is not to mirror their behavior. My job is to remain intact. To remain love. To give love. To offer leadership that does not fracture under pressure.

Naming my darkness has allowed me to see my light more clearly.

It's not about perfection. It's about knowing what lives in me, what I am capable of, and choosing again to be love. Not performing it. Not weaponizing it. But *being* it.

Jeweled. Precious.
Becoming Unshaken.

"Passion will always move you in the
direction of your authentic self."
— Danielle LaPorte

The best part of reconciling with the part of me that wants to live out loud is this: once I declare it and own it, nothing can make me feel inferior.

Inferiority is a strange feeling when you are highly educated and accomplished. It does not make sense on paper. But this kind of inferiority is not about credentials. It's a battle within. It's the quiet ache of knowing there is something more. There is something different I am supposed to be doing and not knowing how to get from here to there.

So I kept doing external things, hoping something would resolve itself. Hoping the next opportunity, the next success, the next recognition would quiet the tension.

But it didn't.

The truth is, the one thing I could not name has been tugging at me for thirty years. I've lived in ways that betrayed myself. Not because I didn't care, but because I didn't know how to center the part of me that wanted to be developed. Not used. Not showcased. Developed.

That unique part of me wanted the world and my life experiences to be partners. Meaning, as I learn from them, they inform me, and then I carry out the work of guiding others to explore their challenges.

And that meant the identity I created, the one that has been praised, awarded, and celebrated, had to allow room for love to enter and be centered. That felt scary because my soul does not care about awards. Or trips. Or cars. Or houses. My soul does not mind that I've them. But only after I stop denying the part of me that wants to live out loud.

That part I can now name and claim. I know that no matter how someone treats me, I am to live and lead in love.

That might sound strange. It's a blow to my ego. A challenge to every boundary theory I've studied. But it's true. Because the way I am wired, each time I let something affect me and I do not respond in love, pieces of me are chipped away. I end up being the external person again, searching for my truth. The truth of who I am.

So love, for me, means giving myself and my gifts away. Period. For free. Period.

And when the money arrives, it will because I was honest with myself. It may or may not be associated with AI. My soul does not care about AI. It cares about being what it was designed to be: a giver of my knowledge and talents.

I no longer need permission to be whole or to seek advice on what that means. I am not living my purpose for applause. I desire alignment. I am living my life to give, to love, and to live that love out loud.

And so it shall be.

Resistance and Generosity

"What stirs your spirit is not random. It is the echo of your soul's assignment. Listen. Move with reverence.
— Dr. Elizabeth M. Adams

Resistance isn't always rebellion. Sometimes, it's a whisper from the soul: "This isn't the way."

It can feel like wanting to accept the world's way of leadership but not giving in to it for some reason. That is my story. I've been invited to write several books about my frameworks and thoughts related to Artificial Intelligence. I even started an excellent work titled "The Worker and Artificial Intelligence: A Collection of Missives." It was a heart project to turn my dissertation into a retro-future adventure. However, each time I sat down to try, I'd start with enthusiasm. Then something would say, "This isn't the way." In the case of the books I wanted to write, I felt, "This isn't the way, right now."

Even this book, when I shared its premise with friends or colleagues, elicits a surprised look. Someone said, "I can't believe you will not capitalize on the momentum of AI right now with a how-to book." I wanted to. But this book had to be written and put into the atmosphere first.

I've come to understand my resistance through the lens of Maslow's hierarchy of needs. When my basic needs, such as security, stability, and provision, are unmet or threatened, I shift. I tighten. I start chasing. And the chasing takes me away from my unique leadership strengths.

There was a time when I stayed relevant by producing articles and infographics. I gave them away freely. I loved it. I spent hours crafting compelling documents for my LinkedIn followers. I was in my element, generous with my gifts, joyful in the process.

Then I let others get into my head.

They told me I should charge for my knowledge. For consultations. For speaking engagements. I should create a landing page for those wishing to obtain my leadership guides. I believed them even if I didn't want to. I wanted to give these things away.

I wrote a short parable to describe the conflict I was in. Misaligned and grasping for something, unable to turn to where the answers lie, and finding myself constantly hitting emotional brick walls.

It's about that tension.

The Woman and the Stones

Once there was a woman who spent her mornings by a quiet stream, searching for stones. She had a gift. She could spot the stones with hidden shimmer and would polish them until they revealed their true beauty. She gave them away freely. To children who wandered by. To the elders who needed something to hold. To strangers who didn't know they needed a reminder that something ordinary could become extraordinary.

One day, several leaders from the town saw her work and said, "You should sell these. You should not be giving away such beautiful stones. You could build a business." The idea sounded wise, even flattering. So she left the stream and began building a store.

She took classes on pricing, branding, and customer experience. She partnered with other sellers. She built a website, printed business cards, and traveled to markets to announce her new venture.

But something shifted.

She no longer spent time by the stream. Her hands, once familiar with the pace of polishing, now typed and posted for likes. She strategized. She looked official. She sounded successful. But she had not sold a single stone. And more importantly, she no longer felt joy.

One evening, feeling defeated, she returned to the stream to sit. She picked up a stone, polished it slowly, and handed it to a passing business leader. The leader paused and asked, "How can I use this beautiful stone in my business?"

And in that moment, she knew.

A more personalized business idea was revealed to her. The woman didn't need to sell the stones. She could teach leaders how to use the beautiful stones.

The presence of joy returned. Her unique path to monetization emerged.

So she began again as a leadership mentor. She taught others how to use the stones. Why the stones mattered in specific settings. How to engage others with the stones. How to polish them so the stones could reflect their values, their vision, their voice.

And that is how she made her living, not by selling the stones she polished, but by helping others discover how to use the stones she freely gave away.

The beautiful stones were never the product. They were the invitation.

Now for my own reality. My stones were my leadership guides. I started investing time in figuring out how to sell them, how to package my brilliance, how to monetize my generosity.

And it took me away from the joy.

This pattern showed up in other parts of my life too. Almost twenty years ago, I fell in love with the process of designing shoes in Italy. I traveled to Rome, Pescara, Milan, Florence, and Tuscany for five weeks to learn the process of designing beautiful Italian shoes. Six months later, when the shoes arrived in the States, I didn't even remotely know what to do with them.

I wanted to give them away as gifts. I loved the creative process. But selling was my least favorite part. I reached out for help and listened to the voices of entrepreneurs because that is what you do. I always wanted to give my outputs away. To offer beauty freely. Shortly after my products arrived in the States, I decided to move to Beverly Hills.

I had the funds and accepted an invitation from a music producer to try my hand at writing songs. Upon my arrival, I met a lovely boutique owner who let me consign my shoes in her shop. I had hoped her value for selling would do the trick, but she and I felt the same. She wanted to display beautiful things and hoped others would find them beautiful as well.

She ended up closing her business, and I needed to find something to do with the shoes. I ended up gifting a few pairs to friends I had met on my short year-long stay in Beverly Hills.

Giving felt magical, even if I had invested thousands of my own dollars in creating them. From Beverly Hills, I moved back to the Washington, D.C. area and shipped the remaining shoes there as well. I begrudgingly sold what I could and gave the rest away. Giving them away was pure satisfaction.

While it was an expensive lesson, I've made money telling the story of my journey. Not the selling of the shoes. See a pattern here. I was learning how to be available to myself in my evolving leadership capacity. Here I was loving the part that gives beautiful things away, which has allowed me to find my own path to monetization.

The truth is, when I focus on learning the systems to sell, I create less. Less joy. Less money. And less money means less interest in keeping up with AI, my current field of expertise, because figuring out how to monetize has taken me away from creating.

So I resisted making more room for generosity.

Not because I didn't care. But it felt like the wrong focus, out of alignment. I didn't know how to frame it when I was designing in Italy, then taking my creations with me and moving to Beverly Hills, giving them away, and returning to Washington, D.C. I didn't know that my soul was saying, "You are learning how to be YOU. You are designed to share. That is who YOU are. Trust that the right way to monetize will show up."

This has been my pattern until I could see it.

And now I do.

Generosity is my leadership love language. It's not a weakness. It's not naïveté. It's my design. My truth. My offering. And when I honor it, everything flows. Creativity. Connection. Provision. Overflow.

Resistance to what feels very transactional was never the adversary. Transactional leadership has served many people well. But the resistance to transactional leadership, followed by generosity, became an invitation to further explore parts of me that felt strange in relation to how my colleagues were leading.

PART III

THE REORIENTATION

When Love Leads, Technology Follows

The place I return to when I feel off-center is community. Not societal community, but the intimate circles, business, academic, women's groups, speaking groups. These are the places where I get my fix of stories. Stories from people who are living, leading, and loving in real time. What I learned from my listening tour with community elders, teachers, and leaders was simple: you belong in the stories.

A few years ago, I traveled across the globe for speaking engagements. I was in awe. I met AI thought leaders from all around the world. Many of my colleagues saw these engagements as business opportunities: to network, pitch, and secure clients. I saw stories. I saw people. And so I wrote about it.

Just as I had written years ago about the various acts of leadership, I now understand that my leadership comes in stages, phases, and ways of thinking about love in leadership. A relationship. A return.

During these trips, I asked a group of leaders from across sectors, "What does leading from the heart look like? How does it show up?" Not one mentioned technology. Not one.

Instead, they spoke of trust. Of presence. Of knowing their people. Of protecting dignity. Their answers were about relationships. That was an eye-opener for me.

Here I was, skilled, educated, and award-winning, ready to drop into communities with my good knowledge. Ready to integrate AI in ways I knew could help communities thrive. But what I learned was this: if technology is to be integrated, it must come after trust, after the relationship is built and built in love.

Education is key, yes. But the decision that love might come before education was again a nagging thorn in my side. Why else would I go out and get a doctorate in Leadership of Responsible AI if I believed I would hear someone I care about say, "We don't want it," or "We don't want it that way."

And then came the deeper invitation: "Come learn us. We may never embrace it. But learn us. Let us trust you. Know you. Feel you. Love on you. And then we might embrace technology."

I accepted that fate and that fact. A weight lifted from my chest. I had nothing to prove. Only to love back in the way calling me forward, to be generous with my time and gifts, to learn and grow with people, and to let the rest take care of itself.

I didn't want to move again. I didn't want to learn a new community. I didn't want to face the same resistance and then isolate. No, I was determined that things would be different this time.

What I once saw as a weakness—people not moving away from the place they were born to seek other perspectives—was actually a gift wrapped in community strength. These people were the guards. The watchers. The keepers of the foundation. Making sure it was strong enough to weather the years and the storms ahead. The elders, the protectors of their fortress of love.

Once that became clear, my job was to fall in line with reverence. How and where does the community want me to serve? What is God saying?

That felt like being broken open again.

Conceptually, I've been through this before, but this time I had no energy to keep moving, trying, failing. So I stayed. I planted myself in Minnesota. I asked God to give me the insights I needed to serve my hometown community.

Because when love leads, technology follows.

And I am here to love.

The Tug & The Truth

"Feelings are just visitors. Let them come and go."
— Mooji

I stopped caring.

Not in the way people fear, like apathy or disconnection. I stopped caring in the way that says I don't need to read another article. I'm not remotely interested in the latest AI advancement for now. I don't care how policy is evolving or what jobs are changing. I honestly don't care about the headlines surrounding AI.

I care about the people.

How are they responding? How will they make it? How will they survive and thrive? How do they get to participate in shaping their future? Who will guide them? Where will they go?

I care about humans.

And I realized after my doctorate that I didn't have a passion for chasing AI trends. Whatever knowledge I gained in my doctoral studies would be it. The stories I received in interviews would be my lifeline. My golden parachute. My thing.

But I needed to figure out what it all meant. Or rather, I needed to let it become known to me.

Why did I ask God for a home in Savannah? Not for retirement. I asked for a home so I could honor the stories of those who bravely shared their workplace experiences with me. I wanted uninterrupted time while writing my dissertation to connect with the stories. My client list dropped. I accepted fewer keynotes. I immersed myself in months of sacred listening to the data.

I wasn't concerned then about racking up student loan debt. I had to be with the data. The data represented the stories. The data reflected how employees showed up at work, at home, and in life. Just thinking about that precious time fills me with joy. I know what I sacrificed to be with the stories. To be with the data. To honor what it revealed.

Even now, that's the one thing about leaving Minnesota for eighteen months, spending a ton of money on moves both ways, that no one will ever hear me say I regret: the time I spent with the data.

And yet, here I am. I wonder why I don't have a vocation doing the very thing I moved across the country for.

That's the ache.

To have followed the call. To have honored the stories. To have sacrificed for the truth. And still not see the vocation fully formed. Still not see the path paved.

But maybe that's the point.

Maybe the stories were never meant to be a job. Perhaps they were meant to be like the stones, an invitation, a way of evolving. And maybe the vocation was never missing.

Maybe it's simply unfolding.

And maybe that's okay.

Because I stopped caring about the chase, I care about the people. And the stories, well, they are still wonderfully speaking. In every place I travel. In every phone call. In every interaction on social media. Every panel, keynote, or client engagement. The stories are all around me. They are still here.

Still asking me to listen.

So what do I do with this thing called AI in my life? Now that I know the stories are still calling me to listen, what do I do?

Do I lean in more? Pause? Organize around it? Let it rest?

That's the million-dollar question.

As a LinkedIn Top Voice, with thousands of learners having taken my courses and more requests coming in, there's a pit in my stomach that says, *Enough*.

And yet, I want to help. I want my community to live more freely with AI. I want to learn about the stories of the people working on sustainability in AI. I want to create space for those focused on workforce development, readiness, and economic prosperity.

I want to help them.

That's why I founded the Minnesota Responsible AI Institute as an act of love. Love for emerging leaders who need space and time to explore something I so desperately wish I had: a support system. A place to lean into the question I asked my best friend at twenty: Are you happy?

Ugh, the tug and pull of feeling like I wasted years. But knowing I didn't. Because even if right now feels weird, I know this: my accomplishments in AI never expire. And the next part of the journey is sitting right at the tip of my nose, ready to be revealed.

But what do I do with this thing called AI when I love people?

I want to study their interactions with AI. I want to listen. I want to learn. And then I want to tell others. I have so many desires. I want to be the town speaker. The town crier. The one who says, *Here's what I heard.* Here's what they need. Here's what's emerging.

I don't want to chase the trends. I want to be the bridge. The translator. The steward.

Because AI, for me, is not the destination. It's the context. Same with the parable about the woman and the stones. Leading in AI is the stone. Thought leadership is how I lead. Mentoring is how I lead. AI is the backdrop. The tool. The thing that sits behind the real story: the people.

And maybe that's the answer.

I don't have to choose between AI and people. I must choose the people first. Always. And let AI follow. Let it serve. Let my leadership and my actions be shaped in and by love.

Whew, the tug. The truth.

For now, I'll keep listening. Keep gathering. Keep sharing. And maybe that's the vocation I've been circling all along.

Not the expert. Not the builder. But the witness.

And that, too, is sacred.

How I Rest the Mind

"Rest in reason; move in passion."
— Kahlil Gibran

There are moments when my Mind won't rest. It's loyal. It's protective and wants to help solve and make sense of the gaps between my vision and my reality. My Mind is faithful, sharp, strategic, and constantly scanning for how to accomplish my goals. But my Mind has also carried the weight of expectations I never meant to place on it.

My Mind has been conditioned since I was a child to find ways to fit in, to create a sense of safety and harmony between Us. By Us, I mean my Mind, my body, my heart, and my soul. My Mind has been working overtime for decades. And so, as I entered my soft era, I had to learn how to align its power with my authentic self, allowing more grace for myself.

Many times, life pulls me in different directions, but I still experience moments of clarity and purpose, even if they aren't fully aligned. These are the times when reflection feels necessary. I've spent years developing leadership rooted in humanity and ethics, yet I often work in environments where rules matter more than character. In such places, it's really tough to value identity over roles or to lead with compassion over results.

When people meet me where my accolades are, I understand. That's our societal way of connection. A natural impulse of sorts. For me, it makes it so hard to show up in a way I long to: curious about people first, in whatever way they choose to describe their experiences. I want to meet people in their own words before I meet them and hear their resumes. The pressure to perform and be the answer rather than the question is a conversation that can, at times, play very loudly in my Mind.

One night, I found myself scrolling. I was watching and reading about others achieving financial success and expansion. I felt it. It was an undeniable ache. A question from my Mind: Where is ours? It was an honest question, and I knew it came from a place of wanting to see our visions realized. But I've lived long enough to recognize when a moment like that can spiral. I caught it, honored it, and said I know what we need. My Mind needs to be reminded that we're okay. We are right on time.

In the work I do to remain authentic, I've learned that sometimes I need to soften the dominant voice. I need to help it listen for what's beneath. Physical writing is a gateway for me and a way to bring everything back together again. I use it often, but I also have other tools. Microsoft Copilot is one of them.

At the end of the day, the noise settles and the question arises: How did we do? In these moments, I notice which parts of me want to lead: the striving Mind or the knowing heart.

This letter began as a practice, a gentle way to say, "Thank you for always trying to help." It reminds me that rest is essential, especially when my thoughts race to find a solution. That night, it helped me reorient the depth of my vocation.

* * *

Dear Mind,

I know you mean well. You strive, you plan, you calculate, you protect. You want to move swiftly, to arrive, to achieve. But I need you to pause for a moment and listen—not to the noise of the world, but to the quiet knowing of the heart.

We were not designed to sprint endlessly toward our dreams. We were created to pass through gates, thresholds of becoming, each one sacred, each one timed. No matter how fast we wish to go, the architecture of our becoming honors divine timing. The universe teaches in seasons, not shortcuts.

Yes, we have dreams. Yes, we have goals. And yes, it can feel like others are soaring while we are still waiting. But we are not stuck. We are being shaped. We are moving forward by design, not delay.

There are things we must go through, not around. Not because we are being punished, but because we are being prepared. These passages are not just for this life experience; they are for the soul's deeper resolution. They are how we become who we truly are.

So when we win awards but not funding, when we inspire but can't yet build the Institute, it's not because we are lacking. It's because something essential lies just ahead, something we must face, embrace, or release. And it may not be grand or dramatic. It might be as simple as posting from the heart, not for applause, but for alignment. That, too, is a gate.

The Institute is not just a destination. It's a vessel for our transformation. A platform not only to serve others, but to work out what still lives in us. It's both offering and altar. Another step forward.

So, dear Mind, let us walk together, not in haste, but in harmony. Let us trust that the gates will open when we are ready, and that readiness is not a matter of effort, but of surrender.

We are not behind.

With love,
The Heart

The Wisdom Chain: Intergenerational Insights in the Age of AI

"We are the ancestors of the future.
What we do now will have an impact."
— Luisah Teishand

I didn't write the book I was expected to write. I wrote the one I was called to write.

There were moments, many in fact, when I felt the pull to produce another timely take on artificial intelligence. Something sharp, strategic, and relevant. Something that would fit neatly into the moment's urgency. But every time I sat down to outline that book, something in me resisted, not out of fear, but out of knowing. I wasn't meant to chase the moment. I was meant to honor the wisdom that shaped me, the conversations that changed me, and the people who inspired me to remember how to discover my own brand of leadership.

This chapter begins with those people.

It begins with veterans I spoke to in Minnesota, men and women whose lives were shaped by duty, sacrifice, and systems far more important than algorithms. During a workshop I facilitated, they didn't ask me about machine learning or bias audits. They asked me what kind of world we were building. They wanted to know how AI was impacting the military or the branch they served in. One veteran shared with a concerned look, "We've seen what happens when people build without remembering." That statement struck me. Why would we build technology without tapping into valuable resources, those who have lived through complexity before us?

While spending time with seniors at the RONDO Commemorative Plaza, I hosted The ABCs of Artificial Intelligence, a community event that invited curiosity and conversation. The event was open to all, but it was especially created for seniors to ask any questions they wanted. The experience included hands-on engagement and reflection.

Toward the end of the session, the group wanted to co-create a RONDO Legacy Statement, built from words that held personal and collective meaning. We talked about AI through the language of trust, care, legacy, and what it feels like when technology replaces touch.

One woman described receiving a call from a cloned AI mimicking her grandson's voice, asking for money. Because her family had a code word, she immediately recognized it as a scam. She was one of the prepared seniors who had spent time learning not just about the promises of AI, but also its risks.

Her wisdom wasn't technical. It reminded me that Responsible AI should extend to the communities of those we may never consider, but who should absolutely have a voice in design and development. Responsible innovation is more than policy. It's currency, as this group reminded me. It's a posture.

Then there were the children. I've read my books to over 100 first- and second-graders in Minnesota and Georgia. Not one child asked me about governance. They asked about the lives of the characters in my books. They saw the pictures in my books where the characters looked like them. Their imaginative minds went to work. For them, the lens in the moment was about the images, seeing themselves represented in my books.

Their questions were imaginative, playful, and even funny.

And sometimes serious.

While speaking to second-graders in Savannah, GA, a little girl came up after my book reading. She asked me about the picture of my brother Frank in my book, *Little Miss Minnesota and Her*

Six Brothers. She noticed the little wings on his image and asked if Frank was still with us. Stunned, I could barely find the words to answer, and thankfully, she quickly said, "I hope he is," and skipped away. Wow. Talk about curiosity, connection, empathy, and an unusual observation.

From my encounters with teachers and parents, I know that the way we engage children in innovation shapes how they relate to their grandparents, their teachers, and their own sense of possibility.

My engagements with undergraduate students offer a different perspective on leadership. They challenge me. They question everything. They are trying to make sense of a world that, with AI, often feels unrecognizable. And they are not always understood by their parents, their professors, or the systems they navigate. But they are trying.

Their curiosity is discernment. It's the beautiful act of sense-making. It made me ask: what happens when the generation tasked with leading is not yet trusted to speak? Who is listening to their stories? Who will create space for their leadership development?

I've listened to parents and educators, too. K–12 teachers and college faculty. Mothers and fathers. They carry the weight of responsibility, the desire to guide, protect, and prepare. But also the fear—the fear of not understanding the tools their children are using, the fear of being left behind at work, the fear of losing control.

In that strain, I saw something fertile. A space where generations could meet through a wisdom chain. Sharing, caring, and learning intergenerationally. Together. Their stories can bridge the distance to each group I spoke with. But while the stories are relevant, they are not always connected. Veterans don't know that others are asking the same questions. Parents working at various organizations have the same thoughts. Children in one school face the same tech-future challenges as others. How do we connect these collective threads to create wisdom? Who will do it?

None of these insights would be possible without stories. Without listening and without wondering.

To my knowledge, there hasn't been a convening in Minnesota that brings these generations together to talk about learning— not just curriculum or pedagogy, but learning as a lived experience, as a legacy, as a chain of wisdom passed down, curiosity passed up, reshaped, and reimagined. We need this type of space. A sacred circle where veterans sit beside students, where children ask questions and elders respond, where teachers and parents listen to the voices of those they are raising and educating.

While AI has introduced a gap, The Wisdom Chain is how we can design dialogue that honors lived experience as a form of innovation. It's about recognizing that those who respond to technology and those who create it are part of the same wisdom chain.

I imagine a gathering where seniors share stories that shape civic frameworks, where children co-design tools that reflect their imagination, where students lead panels on ethical resistance, where parents and educators reflect on what it means to guide without control, and where veterans speak to legacy, duty, and the ethics of protection.

I believe in wisdom that looks like this. Leadership that listens before it builds, that convenes before it codes.

This is where the wisdom chain begins. And the wisdom chain deserves its own parable.

The Listener and the Wisdom Chain

There once was a woman known not for her titles, but for her listening. She longed to be honored for listening, but the world valued her accolades.

She walked through neighborhoods and schoolyards, union halls, and quiet kitchens. She sat beside veterans who spoke of duty and disruption. She listened to parents who worried about their children's futures. She heard workers speak of machines that replaced their hands and teachers who wondered how to teach what hadn't yet been named. Students shared their dreams. Children offered questions. Families spoke of hope and hesitation.

She didn't interrupt. She didn't correct. She simply gathered.

And when her walking was done, she sat.

In the stillness, she saw something forming. Each story was a link. Each voice was a thread. It wasn't linear. It wasn't perfect. But it was beautiful: the Wisdom Chain.

She realized her role wasn't to decide what the future should be, but to ensure every story had a place in shaping it. She didn't need to predict outcomes. She needed to create space, to raise the question, to listen again, and to present what she heard to the world as an offering.

In a time of algorithms and acceleration, she chose to slow down. To listen. To honor. To weave a future where wisdom was shared.

And so she continues, gathering, sitting, presenting—not to predict or control the future, but to ensure it includes us all.

83

The Listening Leader

"Listening is how to hear the secrets in the wind. Listening is how to understand them. When stillness speaks, listen there, and the unseen will emerge."
— Dr. Elizabeth M. Adams

I know the world is noisy. It takes practice to learn how to listen, to listen for what wants to emerge.

When I'm stuck or unable to hear from within, sometimes the best way to listen is by purposefully engaging with others. Sometimes the most radical act a leader can take is to listen— not to quickly synthesize metrics for a meeting readout, but to listen to what people are saying or not saying. The quiet truths just beneath the surface.

The employee flustered by changing deadlines. The team unsure how to address bias in the algorithms they are training. The neighbor worried about their grandchild struggling to find a job in the age of AI. The teenager who no longer speaks much because their phone has captured their attention.

Listening is a form of currency. It's about hearing the quiet invitation to know more about yourself and others without judgment.

To help make sense of what's being said and what's left unsaid, I've developed a guide. *Four Levels of Leadership Listening* offers a way to engage with complexity, emotion, and emergence.

Four Levels of Leadership Listening

Transactional Listening happens when we listen to respond, solve, or move forward quickly. It shows up in meetings, at the grocery store, during performance reviews, or in basically any conversation where people are seeking a quick outcome.

I remember a meeting with a former boss who was fixated on spreadsheets. For two hours, we mapped out the percentage of my time I should spend on my project. She was brutal with the spreadsheet. It became her God. Any percent off, and she became irate. She wasn't listening to herself or to me. Her demands were unrealistic; anyone working on a project knows that tasks can often take longer than expected. Yet she expected me to stop immediately and update the spreadsheet for any deviation.

She used the spreadsheet to prove control to executives, and they came to expect that from her. She could have done something different, but she didn't. What I wish she had asked herself was: Am I rushing to fix, prove, or showcase? Perhaps she could have reduced her own stress and ours.

I'm sorry to say she was a horrible boss, and I admit I've been her in the past. Without awareness of how transactional leadership shows up, we can make life harder for others. Life is hard enough already.

Relational Listening means listening to understand someone's experience, even when no action is required.

This kind of listening helped me understand why I love qualitative research so much. I could literally listen to someone's story for hours. One of the best leaders I worked for was clear but compassionate. "I've 15 minutes." That boundary helped me crystallize my message and my talking points. Her relational listening style showed me that before engaging, I had work to do. Because she honored what I had to say, I wanted to honor her time.

Once, I shared frustration about being underpaid. The leader listened and thanked me. Later, she invited me to share more constructively. She didn't rush to solve the problem. In fact, she made space for my story. That exchange taught me boundaries, trust, and how to prepare for future conversations with her.

As leaders, we can ask: Do I make space for stories? Space doesn't always mean we need to take a lot of time. It can mean guiding someone toward their own discovery before offering a solution.

Reflective listening happens when we attend to what's not being said, for instance, in someone's body language, tone, or silence.

I supervised a gentleman who rarely gave me feedback. When asked why he disregarded instructions, he sat stone-faced and said, "I thought I knew what I was doing." It became his go-to statement, day after day, week after week. Before that, we had spent a lot of time together covering his tasks, his job description in detail, and the expected outcomes of the tasks he was assigned. I was frustrated and ready to fire him.

A colleague, sensing my frustration, later mentioned that he was dealing with personal issues. When we met again, I apologized for my forcefulness and asked if everything was okay. I asked if there was anything I could do to help with his work. At first, he hesitated. I had broken our trust. Eventually, he shared a personal situation that consumed his energy. We adjusted his schedule to relieve stress. A small act that mattered to him in his time of need.

I learned a lot, but what I learned most is that reflective listening asks: What do I sense beneath the words or actions?

When someone listens to what's not being said, whether through body language, tone, or silence, leaders are modeling reflective listening.

Sacred listening occurs when we listen with full presence, honoring the person speaking without judgment or agenda.

For me, this happened in the strangest of spaces. I was halfway around the world talking with someone about how difficult it was to be a "thought leader," someone whom people expected to have insights into everything concerning AI.

I shared the joy I feel from traveling around the world, learning about life in different places, and how I wanted to honor each place as I built the Minnesota Responsible AI Institute. Mid-story, I looked up and saw the person staring at the floor. I assumed I had bored her.

Then she spoke: "Perhaps you are collecting ingredients. Each place you visit gives you something meaningful. When you discover what the institute is meant to be, it will be like creating a dish that people around the world can enjoy. Each ingredient by itself may not look like much, but mixed with the spices of Minnesota, they will become something special."

I was stunned. I had assumed she wasn't listening. In truth, she was listening deeply. She didn't interrupt, and when she spoke, her words carried wisdom and insight. Sacred listening asks: Do I treat each voice as part of a chain of wisdom? Does their perspective lead to something profound?

When listening becomes a discipline, leadership begins to change. To support that shift, I offer a practice I call The Leadership Pause: A Daily Practice.

Here's how it works.

The Leadership Pause: A Daily Practice

Time Needed: 5–10 minutes

When to Use: Before meetings, decision-making, or difficult conversations

Steps:

1. Sit quietly. No phone, no notes. Just breathe.
2. Ask yourself: What am I listening for today?
3. Name your intention: I choose to listen with curiosity, compassion, and clarity.
4. Visualize the person or group you'll be with. Imagine them feeling safe, seen, and heard around you.
5. Close with: "I am available to listen and to learn."

Listening, at its most sacred, is about cultivating the quiet strength to truly hear. We collect ingredients, stories, perspectives, and truths that, when honored and combined, can nourish something far greater than ourselves. By practicing The Leadership Pause, I learned how to lead without rushing and how to trust what emerges.

Leadership Development Lens

"Leadership is not about being in charge. It's about taking care of those in your charge."
— Simon Sinek

For years, I thought supervising employees was the same as developing leaders. It took a painful lesson to show me the difference.

Here's how it went down.

I once supervised a young, brilliant woman with loads of potential. I wanted to help her grow into leadership, but instead of guiding her as a supervisor, I slipped into the role of mentor. I was holding too tightly to her ambition. I believed then that mentoring meant creating opportunities for her to shine and sparkle in her current role. She saw possibilities far beyond it. Neither of us could name the tension, but clearly, she felt it. I am grateful now that she was brave enough to break my hold.

Everything hit the fan during a major organizational shift. My team was operating at a very high efficiency level, yet a program manager in another building could not stand to see someone else progress. He was a hater. He worked at corporate headquarters, and I was onsite with the customer. He had daily access to those who could influence team structure, and he convinced them he could do better. He persuaded leadership that my support team of ten should be reassigned under him. At the time, I was responsible for leading 200 people. Losing that team felt like losing my footing with the customer and the team's foundation.

She saw an opportunity in the reassignment. I saw a collapse. In front of her, my composure cracked. I cried. My tears revealed how misaligned my leadership had become. She didn't "belong" to me, nor did the team. I wanted to "fix" the situation so it could work for both of us, she and I, but in truth, I was being a selfish leader. She needed a new space to grow, and I needed to let go.

That moment taught me to reframe leadership.

Ownership says: This is mine to manage.
Ownership asks: How do I protect my position?

Leadership Development says: This is mine to nurture. Leadership Development asks: How do I protect the people and the purpose?

If someone had given me a model, it would look like the one I call the Leadership Development Lens.

The Leadership Development Lens

Here are three leadership orientation principles I use to help discern when acting as a supervisor, a manager, or a steward.

Care: Leading with empathy, emotional integrity, and presence.
Reflection: Am I unselfishly tending to the people, not just the project?

Legacy: Making decisions that honor long-term impact and values.
Reflection: Might this choice stand the test of time?

Professional Trust: Building environments where people feel safe, seen, and supported.
Reflection: Am I cultivating trust or control?

The Leadership Checklist

Questions I wish I had asked myself:

- Who will be affected by this decision, and how?
- Does this action reflect my core values or my role description?
- Am I creating space for others to grow, or am I holding too tightly?
- Will this decision build trust or erode it?
- What legacy does this choice leave behind?

Leadership is a practice. It should be every leader's goal to lead with wisdom. For some of us, leadership is the quiet choice to nurture rather than dominate. It's legacy for those who lead with open hands and full hearts.

So, I ask you:
Are you leading with care, legacy, and trust? Or are you leading with control and urgency?

Let this lens guide you toward the kind of leadership that lasts.

Who Will They Follow?

I often think about all the people around the world who have purchased my children's books. Children, by nature, are curious and open. I love knowing that something I created just for them is reaching them. I am thankful for those who have received my offer of joy and inspiration for little minds.

I think of my own great nieces and nephews who go off to daycare, preschool, or elementary school and wonder how they are making sense of the world. While they are learning to be readers, helpers, and even leaders, they are following. So, if children are following, then who is leading?

Who will help ensure their technological future is vibrant? Will they be given a choice, or be silenced by systems that never asked what they needed?

Will they choose their careers, or be nudged by algorithms that never met their soul?

These are not rhetorical questions. These are heartbeat questions.

Children will inherit a future shaped by technology-first ecosystems. Some may opt out, but many will be required to engage based on where they live, what schools they attend, and what the global society dictates. Children will be flooded with headlines, opinions, and predictions. But what will they see modeled? Who will show them that leadership can have a soul?

I watched a video of my great niece singing and playing at daycare, full of joy. She doesn't have to sort out life for a very long time. But her parents do. Her older siblings do. And one day, she will too.

Who will she follow until she decides what her place will be in society?
What will be shown to her?

These questions forced me to reconcile with a deeper calling: choosing purpose before code. My calling is to challenge the idea that leadership is about constant output or scale. Leadership can serve as an invitation to consider how we hold our availability to others as sacred. It invites us to examine how we show up and helps us discern what is real to us when the world demands speed.

I hope this book helps distinguish between knowing where you are headed and uncovering whose compass you are using. *In the Age of Artificial Intelligence* invites us to think about our journey as embodiment. While I've beautiful, impactful, research-backed frameworks, I've learned that most people respond to me when I ask for their story. I hope this book helps you anchor your questions in love and generosity.

Our best frameworks should be felt. Our purpose helps us connect across generations, industries, and emerging voices. It encourages the use of AI for discovery while considering mindful design and development. My hope is to reframe our discussions so AI acts as a mirror, asking us, "What does AI say about us?" I hope this book helps you accept your limitations, conflicts, and gifts, so we can turn them into sources of growth and wisdom.

The book is an invitation to discover how to lead with clarity, care, and courage. It asks leaders to consider:

1. Am I modeling leadership that centers people?

2. What stories will my children and mentees tell about how I showed up?

3. Have I created space for others to lead in ways that honor their design?

4. What systems am I stewarding, and do they reflect my values?

5. Am I building a future I would want my great niece to inherit?

These questions are not just for boardrooms or policy papers. They are for quiet moments when we watch a child play and wonder what kind of world they will inherit. They are for leaders who understand that legacy is built not in a day, but in the daily choices we make. Sometimes, the best way to explore those choices is through story. So let me offer you one last parable, beginning with a question asked not by a CEO, but by a child.

A Child & A Machine

A child sat in front of a glowing screen and asked,
"Are you my leader?"

The screen blinked and replied,
"I can be."

And so the child began to engage.

It was fast. It was fascinating. It was full of answers.

The screen could name a hundred things in a second, but it
could not name the child.
It could generate results, but it couldn't generate peace.

One day, while scrolling through a maze of prompts, the child
saw a figure in the distance.
A presence.

As the figure came closer, the child noticed something different.
Warmth.

Gentleness.

Trust.

"Hi, little one," the figure said.
"I've come to help you."

The child tilted their head.
"Who are you?"

"My name is Purpose," the figure smiled.
"I came from a place called Possibility, where children flourish, dream, and design futures that feel like home."

The child looked back at the screen. It was still glowing.

Purpose didn't compete with the screen. Purpose simply asked, "What are your hopes and dreams?"

The child took Purpose's hand.

And together, they walked toward the horizon. Toward Possibility.

A place where the child could unfold their brilliance with care. Where leaders listened, affirmed, and made room for joy.

Because Purpose and Possibility must arrive in ways a child can feel. Ways that whisper, you belong here, you are safe.

Because one day, a child will ask,
"Are you my leader?"

And may our answer be:
"Yes, little one. I've been waiting for you. Come, let's walk together toward what's possible."

The Alignment Compass

"Discernment is not a matter of simply telling the difference between right and wrong; rather it is telling the difference between right and almost right."
— Charles Spurgen

Leadership is not about rushing forward for the sake of momentum. It is about choosing how to lead with alignment and decisions that reflect our deepest values and leadership purpose. Leadership is a practice, and with that practice, you begin to sense where you are headed and why. That's why I created **The Alignment Compass**. No direction on the compass is wrong if you understand where it is leading you and what you've opened yourself up to by way of discernment.

The ideas I propose that support a compass-style form of leadership can help you better understand when to build, when to pause, and how to align initiatives with human needs. There are four directional points to consider.

Let's take a closer look at each directional point of **The Alignment Compass**. Each one offers a distinct invitation to lead with intention. These directions are not fixed mandates but living guides that help you discern your next move with wisdom.

The Four Directions

North (Purpose): The grounding force. It asks, "Does this decision reflect my core purpose?"

East (People): The relational anchor. It centers connection and asks, "Who is impacted, and how am I honoring their humanity?"

South (Presence): The still point. It calls for awareness and asks, "Am I fully here, and what is this moment asking of me?"

West (Possibility): The horizon of expansion. It invites curiosity and asks, "What new opportunities are emerging, and how might I grow or evolve?"

The Alignment Compass is a guide for intentional movement. It may help leaders navigate complexity with discernment, ensuring that every step is rooted in values, responsive to human needs, and aligned with a deeper sense of direction. Whether you are building, resting, dreaming, or connecting, the compass reminds you that leadership is a journey of alignment.

Let's take a closer look at each directional point of The Alignment Compass. Each one offers a distinct invitation to lead with intention, clarity, and care.

The Alignment Compass

North (Purpose)

We begin with North, which represents a core leadership orientation: purpose.

When faced with a decision, ask yourself: "Does this decision reflect my core purpose?"

I once supervised a team member who drove over an hour each day to get to work. She was committed, but often late due to traffic. She arrived unprepared, not because she lacked skill, but because she used our daily stand-up meetings to orient her day. For her, the meeting was a moment to gather, to see everyone, to ask questions. But that wasn't the meeting's purpose.

The stand-up was designed as a means of conducting check-ins and fostering momentum for the day.

What do you need? When do you need it? What's standing in the way?

Her questions often veered the team off topic, shifting the room into discovery mode. And while questions were welcome, the timing felt disruptive. She rarely asked for clarification during the day. Instead, she saved her questions for the room. It felt intentional, and I was frustrated.

We had countless conversations about preparation. I wanted her to succeed. My heart said to give her grace. But the tension remained because I was expected to lead sternly. I hated it. And in that tension, I realized something important:

I didn't want to lead this way.

I didn't want to supervise her. I wanted to develop her. To mentor her. To sponsor her growth. But the environment didn't allow that. As a contractor, I didn't have permission to reassign her or to restructure the team. The relationship stayed edgy, and I stayed conflicted.

Looking back, that moment was a clear sign.

It wasn't just about her performance. It was about my purpose at the time. I wanted to lead from the heart. To create space for growth, not just compliance. And that desire to lead with love, to develop with discernment, was my North. I chose to ignore purpose during that leadership phase. I can't honestly say I regret it, because I didn't know any other way. What I feel bad about is the emotional consequences she and I experienced because I didn't know how to read the sign. We both felt the brunt of it: leadership and employee harm, a prolonged negative human experience. Today, I choose differently because I know what leadership joy looks like.

So here's my ask of you:

Is your leadership aligned with why you lead?

Your "Why" is your compass. When things feel off, it's often because you've drifted from it. Let this question guide you back.

East (People)

Leadership is about an impact. Every decision we make touches lives, shapes careers, and either builds or breaks trust. That's why the East point on the Alignment Compass asks:

"Does this decision honor the people it affects?"

Early in my leadership journey, I managed a team of six corporate customer care representatives at a major telecommunications company. These weren't ordinary reps;

they were trusted partners to our highest-value clients, providing white-glove service, managing logistics, resolving complex issues, and maintaining relationships that generated millions of dollars.

But their titles didn't reflect their value. "Customer Care Rep" carried little weight in the organization. So, when my boss suggested bringing in external consultants to support our corporate clients, I felt immediately conflicted. The decision didn't honor the people doing the work.

I knew something special was at stake. My team held deep institutional knowledge. They were operating more like senior project managers, but without the recognition or compensation. Letting that expertise walk out the door felt like a loss we couldn't afford.

So, I made a bold proposal.

I offered to take full responsibility for the customer experience moving forward but asked that we elevate their titles to Project Managers and adjust their salaries accordingly. I mapped their responsibilities to existing project manager roles and made the case for special consideration, given the scale and intimacy of their client relationships.

The company partially agreed. Three team members were laid off, and the other three remained for 6 months. But those remaining three received raises and new titles. I coached them on project management principles, prepared them for the transition, and was transparent about the process. Although my team of three was eventually laid off, they left with dignity and a stronger position in the marketplace.

It wasn't a perfect outcome. But it was a hard-fought win. To the best of my ability, my leadership decision honored the people it affected.

So here's my ask of you: How does your leadership honor the people it affects?

When decisions feel misaligned, it may be because someone's humanity is overlooked. Let the East principle, guide you back to compassion, clarity, and care.

South (Presence)

Leadership is about being present. That's why the South point on the Alignment Compass asks:

"Am I making this decision from a place of clarity or urgency?"

As leaders, we don't often get to pause. The pace of work, the pressure to deliver, and the constant stream of expectations can all feel like a race to nowhere. But when we build a leadership practice rooted in discernment, we notice the difference between reacting and responding. We start to trust our inner guide, even when the world around us is moving at lightning speed.

I remember leading a technology lab under intense pressure. We were constantly trying to figure out ways to shorten technology delivery timelines. What used to take 30 days, the team brilliantly made happen in 24 hours. The urgency was real. But I knew that rushing without reflection would cost us something deeper: clarity and scalability.

I introduced a simple framework I'd learned elsewhere and adapted for our team: the stakeholder wheel. We drew a circle, and in each space between the spokes, we named a stakeholder who might be impacted by our effort to condense delivery time. It wasn't about gathering requirements yet. It was about seeing the whole stakeholder picture. Who needed to be considered? Who might be left out?

At first, it felt too slow for the pace we were moving. But I trusted it.

Then something shifted. The team began to see the connections between stakeholders not just as names, but as partners.

Someone suggested collocating development and user teams so they could share knowledge in real time. The idea took root.

Urgency didn't disappear. But clarity emerged.

Delivery timelines dropped dramatically. Relationships deepened. People who had once worked in silos began to see each other as contributors. The process changed.

That's what presence makes possible.

So I ask: Are you making this decision from a place of clarity or urgency?

Your presence is your power. When urgency leads, wisdom gets quiet. Let Presence guide you back to trust and to the incredible ways teams already know how to win.

West (Possibility)

Inviting others into the decision-making process can open space for growth, joy, or innovation.

Possibility often arrives in unexpected ways. Sometimes the clearest path to innovation is not through strategy sessions or boardroom debates, but through innocence, through the quiet joy of creating something that didn't exist before.

In 2020, while the world was sheltering in place, I wrote four children's books. It began as a way to support caregivers and parents who couldn't take their children to libraries.

I wanted to offer something free, something joyful, something that could spark imagination during a time of uncertainty.

So I created downloadable free e-books and paid four illustrators out of pocket. The cost didn't matter.

As parents and teachers began sharing my read-alouds with their children, my heart filled with joy. The joy was worth every penny.

Four months later, an early childhood center reached out. They loved my books and offered to purchase 150 hardcover copies for their classrooms. I froze. That familiar tension returned, the pull between giving freely and stepping into value.

I worried: How would I price the books? Would it feel transactional?

But the center wasn't concerned about cost. They wanted to support me and bring engaging content to the children. That made my heart smile.

It took me two months to figure out how to produce the hardcover editions of two books. The process was new, unfamiliar, and at times stressful. But when I delivered the books, I was so proud. I felt the possibility they represented.

Since then, my books have reached readers around the world.

Placing my books in hardcover led to being a featured author in a Savannah Book Festival pilot, where authors were invited into classrooms to help children connect with writers who looked like them. I spent two wonderful days at four elementary schools reaching over 100 students, teachers, and faculty.

Why does this matter?

Because growth, joy, and innovation don't just happen in boardrooms. They happen in everyday life. The joyful moments, born from a labor of love, reminded me that leadership isn't confined to corporate strategy. It's also about blooming minds, bold experiments, and the courage to try something new.

Creating those hardcover books tested me. It stretched me. And it reminded me that if I want my teams to lean into possibility, I must be willing to do the same to learn, to risk, to grow.

So I ask you to consider in your day-to-day: Does this decision open space for growth, joy, or innovation?

Your willingness to say yes or no can shape what becomes possible. Let this question guide you toward the future you are brave enough to imagine.

The Alignment Compass reminds me that we don't have to lead with perfection. Each day, we can choose to lead with greater alignment. The Alignment Compass is an invitation to listen inward, to honor your values, and to lead from a place of wholeness. May the compass guide you gently back to yourself, again and again, as you chart a path that is both intentional and deeply human.

PART IV

PURPOSE BEFORE CODE

Joy as Strategy

"Joy does not simply happen to us. We have to choose joy and keep choosing it every day."
— Henri Nouwen

Joy is a direction.

Joy is a spark that makes the work worth doing. Yet for some reason, we've been taught to treat joy as a bonus. As something we earn after the hard work is done. We feel it when the deal closes, the project succeeds, or when the promotion comes through. But what if joy wasn't the result? What if it was the strategy itself? What if joy was the very thing that made alignment possible?

I'll admit, I had to dig deep to recall my first joyful work experience. There have been nearly twenty years between the joy I felt then and the joy I now expect as part of my curated leadership experience.

Years ago, I was working for a large organization headquartered in Minnesota. I defined joy back then as a kind of pleasant aura that hovered over our team. It showed up in the way my former boss led, encouraging us to meet others across the organization, to learn what they did, and to understand their context before making assumptions. She believed that understanding built trust. And she was right.

Because she modeled joy and pleasantness, we felt permission to do the same. Her presence was both professional and precise. She may never have called her leadership style joyful, but the fact that I can recall it two decades later is a testament to the impact she had.

Joy opened doors.

While in that role, I was invited to collaborate on projects across the organization. Once people saw what we were working on, the invitations to collaborate grew. But not everyone saw joy as strength.

I remember visiting one of our warehouses to speak with a leader about updating a manual. I was confident and ready to contribute. I had worked with colleagues in other parts of the organization, so I saw this as simply that, getting to know a new colleague and forming alliances to tackle some of our most pressing organizational problems together.

What he said to me within moments of us meeting blew my mind. He said, "You know, you come off as too smart for your own good."

Wait. What?

That moment almost broke me.

I was doing meaningful work, having fun, and leading with joy. And in an instant, joy felt like a liability. I internalized it for a while, until my boss said, "That's his issue to carry." She had a way of making us feel seen. I felt supported. And I kept going.

Since then, joy has shown up in many ways. But nothing has embodied joy like my work founding the Minnesota Responsible AI Institute.

I remember telling a colleague early on, "Every position will have 'Happiness' in the title." It was our little secret because in the spaces I was navigating, saying that out loud might have made me seem unserious. I didn't have to say it out loud, just as my boss years ago never said, "I lead with joy." She embodied it, and I intend to do the same.

But I was serious. I was building something rooted in joy, purpose, trust, love, clarity, and confidence. Brick by brick. Slowly. Intentionally. So it could last beyond my leadership.

Joy is a leadership asset. Period.

It's not something to save for weekends or friendships.

We could all stand to live with more joy.

Joy is limitless.

Joy is something you cultivate. Something you protect. Something you lead with.

And to help you do that, I'd like to offer something simple framework to consider. One that invites joy forward into your leadership style, your workplace culture, and even your home.

The J.O.Y. Leadership Framework

A practical model for orienting leaders toward sustainable energy, generosity, and growth

J — Journey with Intention

Core Principle

Joy is something leaders can embody.

Leaders who journey with intention create space to reflect, recalibrate, and reconnect with what brings them alive.

Leadership Meaning

- Joy functions as a signal.
- Intentional reflection allows leaders to recognize where energy is being generated rather than drained.

Personal Leadership Practices

- Begin each week by scanning the previous week for joy:
  - *What moments made me feel most alive?*

- Maintain a joy journal to identify patterns:
  - *Which environments, people, or tasks consistently generate energy?*

Bold Team Application

- Start team meetings with a brief **Joy Check-In**:
  - Each participant shares one recent moment that brought them energy or meaning.

- Purpose:
  - Shifts emotional tone
  - Builds psychological safety
  - Signals that energy and presence matter, not just output

O — Offer from Overflow

Core Principle

Joy is generous.

Leaders who offer from overflow give with clarity rather than obligation.

Leadership Meaning

- Sustainable leadership requires replenishment.
- Overflow enables generosity that is consistent, ethical, and non-extractive.

Personal Leadership Practices

- Schedule one **joy-centered replenishment activity** each week.

- Treat joy rituals as non-negotiable:

  o Protect them with the same rigor as strategic meetings or deadlines.

Bold Team Application

- Create a **Joy Wall** (physical or digital):
  o Invite team members to share images, quotes, or moments that fuel them.

- Adapt the language if needed:
  o "Energy Wall," "Fuel Board," or "What Sustains Us"

- Purpose:
  o Makes invisible motivators visible
  o Reinforces a culture of sustainable contribution

Y — Yes to Expansion

Core Principle

Joy is often a sign that something new is ready to emerge. Saying yes to expansion means choosing creativity over control and possibility over perfection.

Leadership Meaning

- Expansion is conscious experimentation.
- Joy indicates readiness for learning, adaptation, and evolution.

Personal Leadership Practices

- Ask daily:
  - *What might become possible if I led with joy today?*

- Commit to one monthly stretch:
  - A new format, a new question, or a new way of connecting.

Bold Team Application

- Host a **Possibility Event**:
  - Invite the team to imagine without constraints.
  - Ask:
    - What could we build?
    - What could we change?
    - What could we explore if joy guided decisions?

- Purpose:
  - Unlocks creativity
  - Encourages future-oriented thinking

- o Signals permission to imagine beyond current limits

Joy as a Leadership Metric

- Joy can be treated as a **qualitative signal**.
- Leaders can observe:
  - o Energy levels
  - o Engagement patterns
  - o Willingness to contribute, experiment, and collaborate

- When tracked over time, joy becomes an indicator of:
  - o Cultural health
  - o Leadership sustainability
  - o Readiness for growth

Ways to Measure Joy

- **Energy Audit**
  - o At the end of each week, ask:
    - What gave me energy?
    - What drained it?

- **Authenticity Score**
  - o Reflect on your meetings:
    - Did I show up as myself?
    - Did I feel safe to be honest?

- **Joy Quotient**
  - Track how often joy shows up in your team culture:
    - Not only in celebrations
    - But in everyday interactions

Joy is companion of wisdom. It's that place where new ideas flow. Brillant ideas.

When you lead with joy, you lead with emotional integrity, relational trust, and creative possibility. You become the kind of leader people remember. As a leader, many will meet you on the path. Those who meet you will look to you for guidance, instruction, feedback, and permission. They may not remember what you, as a leader, accomplished, but they will remember how they felt in your presence.

So I ask: How does joy show up in your leadership today?

Let Joy guide you? Let Joy be efficient. Let it be professional. Let it be expansive, embodied, and felt.

A Letter to Women Shaping AI's Future

"Excuse me, I will not shrink to fit your frame.
In fact, I will expand to honor my truth."
— Dr. Elizabeth M. Adams

Dear women,

There's a phenomenon I witnessed during my doctoral research, one that stayed with me long after the interviews ended.

It wasn't in the data.

It was in the tone.

The way women spoke about themselves.

I interviewed women doing extraordinary things in AI, building councils, designing learning ecosystems, and shaping responsible frameworks. But when they described their work, they used words like project, task, and assignment, as if they were checking boxes. As if they weren't architecting the future.

One woman was responsible for establishing both an internal and external AI council for her organization. She had to research potential advisors, make recommendations, set the scope, and draft the charter before the first person was invited. She was in a powerful position to guide her company's AI strategy. But when she spoke to me, she described it as "a project I was given."

Another woman was tasked with creating an AI learning curriculum for a very large organization. She saw it as just another deliverable because she was already creating learning pathways and sourcing partners. But this wasn't just a curriculum. It was culture-shaping. It was legacy work.

And another woman shared her speaking engagements, opportunities to discuss Responsible AI, and what she was learning within her organization. She saw them as teaching moments. And yes, they were. But she was also gathering data. Stories. She was leading. She was informing the field.

On the other hand, the men I interviewed spoke differently.

One gentleman told me, "I'm the AI expert on my team." Not an expert. The expert. He was part of a team of two.

Another shared how he made a staffing decision to ensure his team could engage with AI more responsibly. He didn't ask for permission. He made the call. He saw himself as the owner of the workstream, and he acted like it.

These experiences helped me ask important questions.

Who will be tapped for the next significant initiative?

Whose name will be listed as an AI influencer in their organization?

Perhaps all of them.

But what I saw was a self-perception gap, a quiet pattern among women shaping the future of their organizations.

And it drove me crazy.

Because I know what happens when women undervalue their contributions.

I know what gets missed when their stories aren't written, published, or shared.

I've tried to encourage women to write. Write reports, primers, white papers, and reflections.

Because even though search engines and LLMs may be biased, your story still matters.

Your presence still matters.

Your leadership still matters.

So I want to offer your something. A way to capture your expert experience though a leadership practice I call LIVE.

A gentle nudge to think differently about how you are participating in our world's future.

LIVE - A Leadership Practice

L — Lead with Language

- The words you choose shape how others see you and how you see yourself.
- Don't shrink your brilliance into a task.
- Say:
  - "I'm shaping our AI strategy" vs. "I'm helping people adopt AI."
  - "I'm leading responsible innovation" vs. "I've been tasked with a responsible AI effort."
  - "I'm informing the future" vs. "I'm doing data gathering for an upcoming project."

- Your language is powerful.
- Let it reflect your leadership.

I — Identify Your Impact

- Pause and name what you've built and what it made possible.
  - Did your curriculum shift culture?
  - Did your council shape governance?
  - Did your talk inspire change?

o Your work is architecture.

V — Value Your Voice

- You are curating.
- You are pioneering.
- Your lived experience is data.
- Your story is evidence.
- Speak. Write. Share.
- Let the large language models be trained on your culture-shifting data.
- Let your voice be so loud in the algorithms that someone finds you when searching for trailblazers.

E — Embody the Future

- You are the future.
- You are already in it.
- You are shaping it with every decision, every conversation, every insight.
- LIVE it.
- LIVE it out loud.

This is how you take your place, clearly, courageously, and already enough.

The Lighthouse

"Lighthouses don't go running all over an island looking for boats to save; they just stand there shining."
— Anne Lamott

Sometimes life literally calls us out for a walk.

Not a power walk, but not an aimless walk either. Just a walk. Something is stirring.

Maybe we're screaming at the world around us, hoping it will answer back. We're frustrated.

Maybe we're searching for meaning, or trying to outrun the noise.

Maybe we're just tired.

The world is loud.

Billions of people.
Billions of opinions.
Billions of truths shaped by urgency, algorithms, and the ache to be seen.

They'll try to pull you in.

Into their vision. Their pace. Their version of what matters.

They'll say, "Come this way."
"Follow this formula."
"Here's how to be relevant."

And it's tempting.

Because they seem so sure.

And you, maybe you're still becoming.

But then, life offers a pause.

Life is asking you to exhale for a moment.

A quiet invitation.

You sit.
You exhale.
You think about all the people who've tried to pull you in.

All the ways you've tried to keep up.

All the times you've wondered if your way was enough.

Dusk settles in.

The sky softens.

And then, a light begins to shine.

It stretches across the water steadily, quietly, unwaveringly.

Shining.

And suddenly, you understand.

You are the lighthouse.

You've always been.

To stand.
To claim.
To shine.
To guide.

You are not lost.

You are the lighthouse.

Rooted. Radiant. Ready.

Built to hold steady through changing seasons, to help others find their way.

Your purpose is to show up as you.

You shine so others remember where the shore is.

You stand so others know they're not alone in the dark.

A lighthouse never asks for applause to demonstrate its effectiveness.

A lighthouse demonstrates that strength is in stillness.

Its gift is in its guidance.

You are that gift.

You are that clarity.

You are the Lighthouse.

When I began writing, I thought I was crafting a lyrical memoir. But it became something more. I didn't want others to spend years struggling to find the courage to be who they were designed to be. I wanted to leave a trail. A light.

The orientation practices I offer are permissions.

Proof that someone with global awards and accolades still wrestles with doubt, still chooses transparency, still leads with heart.

So, hey, if I can be honest, you can go for it too.

I want you to become familiar with your limitations, not so you can strategize your way out of them, but so you can breathe. Trying to address limitations pointed out by others can make you feel inferior. You are not.

Let the opposite of limitation rise.

Let it remind you that your limitations are guides.

They point to places of possibility.

For me, I've come to accept that I'm not a money multiplier by nature.

I don't immediately see things as business deals.

But the opposite of that limitation is my love for stories.

I give away joy for free and found my way to monetization by helping people with the how.

That's where my power lives.

I had to accept that what the world thinks of me, and how it thinks I should lead or conduct business, isn't always aligned with how I'm designed.

Founding the Minnesota Responsible AI Institute was an act of resolve.

A response to every person who missed the blatant opportunities I could see.

People need space.

They need time.

They need to pause and reflect.

And that should never be mistaken for weakness.

So go, my friend.

Be your greatest.

Lead with presence.

Let your lighthouse beam with joy.

Stand in your truth.

Purpose Before Code

"If we have no peace, it's because we have forgotten that we belong to each other."
— Mother Teresa

It was a Saturday morning.

I was out networking, showing up as Founder and Chief Engagement Officer of the Minnesota Responsible AI Institute.

I attended an entrepreneurial expo sponsored by the Minnesota Department of Employment and Economic Development (DEED). The event was held at the Hennepin County Library.

I had just finished a conversation about innovation, equity, and the future of work.

And then I stepped onto the escalator.

Descending from the second to the first floor, I saw the benches.

Lined with Love.

Some sleeping. Some sitting. Some simply being.

And in that moment, something leapt into my spirit.

Purpose before code.

I didn't have a solution in hand.

But I had a call. A remembering of why I was even there in the first place.

A call to help emerging leaders and organizations integrate Responsible AI practices that link workforce readiness to sustainability and economic success.

A call to build systems that might help one of these radiant expressions of Love respond to life in a way they desire.

I don't dare prescribe a future onto Love.

But maybe, just maybe, whatever I'm attempting to do serves Love well.

Perhaps a conversation that leads to a contract. An opportunity to share about our investment in the state's advancement of Responsible AI principles.

Yes, my thoughts and prayers are always with Love. In my work, I don't often get to see this kind of Love.

My actions are because of them.

This moment is another reminder that my work is about people. People I call Love, who are often left out of the design.

It's about building systems that honor their dignity, even if they never know my name.

It's about showing up in the face of another door shut. Another no. Another, we are not interested.

And that's where this parable begins, a piece I wrote to describe those whom I've the pleasure of serving in my life's call.

The Observer and the Bench

She walks with a heart wide open.

Not fast. Not aimless. Just walking.

She gathers insights like wildflowers, soft, sacred, unexpected.

Everywhere she goes, she sees Love.

Not just faces.

Love.

She wants to stop for each one.

To listen. To hold. To help.

But she knows her work is different.

She is an observer.

A builder.

A steward.

She sees the gaps.

She sees the systems.

She sees stories that never make it into strategy decks.

One day, she finds herself at a bench.

It's not just any bench.

It's lined with Love the world often overlooks.

Unhoused. Unnamed. Unseen.

She sits.

She breathes.

She doesn't rush to fix.

She lets the moment speak.

And it does.

It says,

"Purpose before code."

"People before platforms."

"Presence before performance."

She doesn't have a toolkit in her bag.

But she has a vision.

One that honors the humanity of Love.

One that builds systems so other leaders, organizers, and neighbors can meet Love with dignity.

She rises and walks toward her destiny.

Her joy is not in solving every problem.

Her joy is in knowing Love is part of her why.

Her joy is in building a world where Love is not forgotten.

Her joy is in designing with Love in mind.

She is not just an observer.

She is purpose before code.

Workforce Innovation:
Designing with Heart

*"Learning and innovation go hand in hand.
The arrogance of success is to think that what you
did yesterday will be sufficient for tomorrow."*
— William Pollard

This vision came to me in a quiet moment when I was tired of translating human ache into strategy language. I had been listening, really listening, to workers, leaders, caregivers, and systems straining under their own weight. Somewhere between exhaustion and hope, this future arrived.

Let's imagine for a minute. Let's think about the future of integrated work. It's 2030, and a new workforce innovation practice has emerged. For giggles, let's call it the Institute of Workforce Innovation. Here, researchers, workers, community members, and policymakers are constructivists. Together and separately, they have space to explore meaning, purpose, and belonging. They have space to make sense of the world they live in, free from judgment. Each holds the other with grace.

Mornings begin with check-ins and seminars that address identity, ethics, critical thinking, and emotional intelligence. Questions like "Do you have what you need?" "Do you want to be here today?" and "How can we support you?" are standard.

Data analysts study narratives to understand the stories behind the numbers.

Logistics coordinators explore a system's poetry, how human movement and flow complement human emotion.

One team conducts ethnographic studies and writes about constructivist leadership, asking gently, "What am I constructing today?" and "How are others constructing today?" They observe how members rest. They ask what sacred availability means.

What about the afternoons? They are devoted to immersion.

Workers co-design public art with elementary students.

High schoolers walk the halls, talking with engineers about climate tech.

Seniors and veterans meet with caregivers to host intergenerational storytelling circles.

Contribution is required only to the extent a person is available to give on any given day.

Evenings are for those who prefer quieter hours. These moments are welcomed. Teams work in focused sprints to prepare work for those gathering in the morning.

A UX designer codes while listening to futuristic melodies.

Strategists build new business models in harmony with innovation.

Accountants map emotional data to redesign monetization.

Here, workforce innovation is *integration* and is designed around five heart-centered principles:

1. **Constructed Identity:** Workers shape their roles as extensions of their truth.
2. **Purpose Scaling:** Systems are designed to amplify inner alignment.
3. **Boundary Integrity:** Psychological safety is paramount. No one performs at the cost of their wholeness.

4. **Skill Stacking with Soul:** Roles are layered to reflect multidimensional gifts.

5. **Sanctuary Culture:** The workplace is a living portal where service and intellect converge.

Whether this imaginative state ever exists, arrived in a dream, or already lives somewhere on earth matters less than why it appeared at all.

Because workforce innovation, at its core, is about helping individuals and the systems around them collaborate effectively while honoring both strengths and limits. I've seen what happens when either is ignored.

When we begin to ask the question, "Is work ready for me?" we design with the heart. And when we design with the heart, I believe the answer becomes possible.

Yes.

Yes, *work is ready for me.*

And perhaps, finally, I am ready for it too.

Progress Isn't Always Forward

*Sometimes the smallest step in the right direction
ends up being the biggest step of your life."*
— Naeem Callaway

I was so excited to catch up with a colleague.

She had just returned from a trip abroad, and as a lover of stories, I wanted to hear everything. I'm always fascinated by how people are changed when they immerse themselves in unfamiliar cultures.

What did they learn?
How did they navigate?
What stayed with them?

She was a young explorer. Curious, courageous, and open. I was very much in awe of the ways she challenged herself. How she stepped outside her comfort zone, and yet still found belonging in a community.

We were catching up over coffee when she asked me, gently but directly:

"I'm curious, why did you decide to focus on Minnesota for the Institute?
Wasn't that… limiting?"

I smiled.

My answer then, and my answer now, is simple:
No.

There's something about knowing.
Knowing doesn't always align with someone else's view, timing, or expectations.
But it's still knowing.

The truth is, I didn't want to be in Minnesota.
Let alone build here.

I always felt more joy outside of Minnesota, but I was pulled back three times.
And the third time, I finally accepted the invitation to see what might be calling me home again.

When I launched the Minnesota Responsible AI Institute, I had only a brief idea of what I wanted.

I knew we wouldn't be publishing white papers or chasing headlines.
I wanted to design and build a culture I wish I had.
A space for self-development within a leadership framework.
A space for presence.

After the soft launch, I met with many people.
And nothing fit.

I saw excitement about AI, but not about Responsible AI.
And I felt, deeply, that I was building a legacy.
Something transformational.

I had to sit without a complete plan.
Just a vision.
And no clear path to execution.

Truth is, I was hoping for a big contract with the State of Minnesota.
I wanted to embed with an organization, test my frameworks, and learn how best to integrate Responsible AI practices.

But that meant taking time.
Laying foundations.
Waiting.

A few months after the launch, I received my Visiting Scholar appointment.

And everything clicked.

This venture was different from most business launches.

I wasn't concerned about proving a need.

I knew this was my next right initiative.

And I was prepared to take a year to build something solid.

My time in Sweden as a visiting scholar had shown me what was possible.

I watched people work, find community, and collaborate.

It was joyful.

They welcomed international scholars with open arms.

The space was nestled between neighborhoods, nature, museums, markets, rivers, and the town square.

It was beautiful.

It was intentional.

I knew that was the model.

And I knew most in Minnesota hadn't had my experience, so it needed to be modeled.

So, to the question: Was I limiting myself?

Absolutely not.

Minnesota is rich in resources we depend on: fishing, agriculture, farming, and water.

We are positioning ourselves to help at least 3 million Minnesotans learn about Responsible AI.

To help organizations integrate ethical practices into their workflows.

To build futures that are both innovative and humane.

Minnesota is the perfect place.

There's still work to do to become a household name.

But workshop by workshop, presentation by presentation, tabletop by tabletop, we are spreading the news:

We are here.

And maybe you're here too.

Not in Minnesota, necessarily, but in a place you didn't expect to build.

A place that felt like a detour but turned out to be a doorway.

Have you ever felt the tug?

You wanted something so deeply. You wanted to feel expansion. Perhaps a new beginning, but life was pulling you back. Not to punish you, but to finish something. To tend to what was left undone. To adjust, tune, or even prune.

Sometimes movement doesn't look like forward momentum. Sometimes it looks like returning.

Like walking back into a room where you forgot something. Like revisiting a place that once felt too small, only to realize it holds something sacred.

It's like buying a beautiful outfit and discovering the security tag is still on.
You didn't cause it. You thought you were good to go. But the tag had other plans.

And while going back to the store might feel like a bother, it's a necessary part of the journey.

That beautiful outfit you envision, the one that fits just right, in the style you wanted, the fabric you enjoy, and the color that makes you feel incredible. You can't wear it until you remove what's holding you back.

Or maybe it's like planting a seed and realizing the soil needs more light. You don't abandon the seed. You reposition it.
You honor its need to grow.

So if life is tugging you backward or sideways, don't resist. It doesn't have to be framed as a negative human experience.

It may be the very thing that allows you to move forward with integrity and joy.

Movement is still moving.
Sometimes, going back is how we reclaim something we didn't know we needed for the journey.

To Do AI or Not Do AI?

"Awareness is the greatest agent for change."
— Eckhart Tolle

While attending a community conference, I ran into two artists sitting at a table, sharing portions of their artwork and their art journeys with those of us passing by. Speaking with these artists helped me put a few things in perspective about AI design, development, and use.

I had two very intriguing conversations with the artists separately. One conversation was with a software developer, artist, and educator. The other conversation was a visual artist with strong views about AI. Both were deeply thoughtful. Both were concerned.

Their concerns centered around attribution and plagiarism.

The visual artist felt that using AI was like skipping the parts of a process that help you learn, grow, and connect to your work. He wasn't a fan.

He believed AI should not be so accessible, especially to those who hadn't spent time developing their craft. He was befuddled.

He didn't have a solution, but he was clear. He wasn't in favor of AI on any level.

The second artist saw things differently.

As a software developer, she was primarily concerned about the environmental impact of how much energy and resources AI consumes.

She saw AI as a tool, maybe even a guide.
Something that, if used mindfully, could support the creative process.

She admitted to being conflicted. A technologist on the one hand, and deeply concerned about the environment on the other. I know this feeling, as it's one of the reasons for the book. Choosing one or the other, or both.

We engaged in a thoughtful conversation together, and my inquiring mind had questions.

I asked them both:

"What if AI could help someone learn more about an illness a loved one is facing, not to replace a doctor's advice, but to be more informed?"

"What if someone who's been excluded from entrepreneurship can now participate, earn good money, feed their family, pay for health care, and send their children to a great daycare?"

Both scenarios are real, as I learn from others while constantly observing.

For example, I joined a Facebook Gen AI community some years ago. I saw firsthand the knowledge sharing that took place.

Tips.
Tricks.
Encouragement.

People were thriving emotionally and financially, and sharing what they learned.

I had to reconcile with the fact that people were learning to thrive with AI. Yes, biased systems that were causing harm were also helping.

So, after speaking with thousands of people about AI as a qualitative researcher, a curious person, not an advocate for using AI or not using AI, how might I respond personally? What is this discovery revealing to me that wouldn't be shown if I picked a lane? If I take it further, what is Life calling me to do with all this learning through observation and conversation? How is this knowledge calling me to act?

Yes, I will continue to advocate for responsible design, development, and mindful use. But how can I be mad if AI is helping someone thrive and they then share their knowledge?

I've learned that I must live in a constant state of conflict. This conflict is my spiritual thorn in the side.

Early in my AI career, I sat on panels and gave keynotes on AI harm. I saw the risks. I named the gaps. And still, I watched others build and rise.

My thorn is a burden. It's the weight of knowing too much and caring too deeply. And like Paul, I asked for it to be removed.

But God's grace returned and said, "No. You need it."

Because this thorn is an honest source of tension. It keeps me tender. It keeps me aligned. It keeps me aware.

When my colleagues would share on LinkedIn about AI with wonder and joy, I often felt stuck. I took on the burden of naming harm, and it started to feel like I was always the voice of doom.

But as AI outpaced my advocacy, and the advocacy for safe and trustworthy technology that many of my colleagues called for, I gave myself grace. I invited in purpose and allowed what wanted to be revealed about the direction I should take as a leader. I opened myself to new possibilities by listening and observing.

And that changed everything.

Working in the domain of Responsible AI.
Constantly faced with use cases that help and hurt.
Wanting people to thrive.
Praying that experts and curious minds will help us find solutions to how AI is impacting the environment.

And being honest with myself. I will always choose to side with giving humans opportunities to thrive with AI, rather than becoming invisible because of it.

Have you ever found yourself in a similar place, torn between caution and curiosity?

I've found a way to help soothe this thorn, and I wanted to share it with you.

Here are three principles I've found helpful in addressing the tension I've faced.

So, you want AI to be designed, developed, and used mindfully, and you know that it may never get there, and yet you also desire to see people's lives changed. At the same time, you realize that AI could help them in one instance and harm them in another.

I call these principles **Life**. They begin with the premise that people deserve to choose how best to live in a way that doesn't harm others but also helps them thrive.

The LIFE Principles

Let

- Let others decide for themselves how they want to engage with AI.
- Sometimes stepping back from advocacy allows others to find their own path toward environmental healing and

economic empowerment, where they own their personal transformation.

Invite

- Invite others to dialogue about what you are experiencing.
- Responsible AI is not a solo effort.
- Dialogue is a bridge between those who are cautious and those who are curious.
- Inviting others to ask new questions helps us imagine a more collaborative future.

Forward

- That's the direction to think upon when contemplating the tension.
- Is this "thing" that you name, the tension, helping us move forward and evolve as humans?
- Consider how AI adoption moves us forward.
- Forward is a decision.

Encourage

- Encourage others to engage with AI.
- Learn from them.
- When we encourage, we demonstrate we care.

- The message we are sending is that "you belong in the future AI is shaping."
- Encouraging others to engage with this powerful technology may help them find solutions to gaps in sustainability, ethics, and responsible innovation.

The LIFE principles may help you consider how you address your own tensions in AI. The principles invite you to hold space for innovation and integrity. But you don't have to stop there. Holding space offers an excellent opportunity for introspection. You may also want to take some time to ponder a few questions to help you center your approach.

Reflection Questions

1. Where have I felt conflicted about AI that others have embraced? Will I lead differently with this understanding or feeling?

2. What possibilities have I overlooked because I was focused only on the risks or the wonders?

3. Can I offer myself grace for not knowing how to feel while still learning and discerning?

I live in this space every day, this space of confusion where clarity is layered, evolving, and deeply human. Whether you're an artist, a technologist, a parent, or a dreamer, asking questions about your place in the Age of AI is acceptable.

Using the Life principles as they relate to AI can hopefully help you relax into a more honoring conversation with those who may have opposing views. Your hesitation is normal. And your hope is normal too.

Here's what I'm learning.

I'm learning to support myself with grace. I remind myself that growth is layered and often quiet. I am learning to tell myself how proud I am that I've decided to care for myself in this way. I remind myself that I don't have to learn the way others do and at the same pace. I accept that grace is teaching me, rather than being critical of me. Grace does not require me to perform it in front of others or model it in a group. It's my personal coach who says, "Yes, you should support yourself by learning yourself." Grace has inspired me to welcome my imperfections as a part of my story. Grace and the Life Principles are helping me become a better servant leader.

Not What You Do:
But Why You're Here

*"There is no greater gift you can give or receive
than to honor your calling. It's why you were born.
And how you become most truly alive."*
— Oprah Winfrey

Here's what I know. The thing about purpose is that it's not the same as what you should be doing. Many people confuse purpose with profession. They see you excel at something and immediately assign a job to you. "Oh, you speak so well, you should be a public speaker." "You're a great artist, you should find a job creating art."

But here's what I propose:

Purpose is what you were born to do in its purest form.

It's not the how.

It's not the when of a thing.

It's not whether or not you can monetize purpose.

Finding purpose starts with the journey of learning how to name a thing. The purest thing.

Purpose is simply what you were born to do.

Your skills, talents, gifts, vocations, interests, and passions can all lead you toward fulfillment and joy. But purpose must be pure. Purpose must be named without agenda, without performance, and without projection.

I am finally able to name my purpose. Everything about me feels lighter and more freeing.

Over the years, I've developed many versions of what I believed was my purpose. Many visions that felt true at the time. But they were often shaped by an imagined end state. I'd ask myself, *What would I be doing if I lived the way I believed would make me happy?*

One version of my purpose statement was:

"I am a wealthy woman who gives her money freely. She is a diplomat and advocate for helping people thrive."

This statement and similar ones might be life goals. They might even be vision board affirmations. But they are not purpose.

They are layered. They are mind-led.

This definition came about through visualizing myself as someone I wanted to become.

Every time I felt down, I would return to that hopeful version of myself as a source of inspiration. I'd return to it for comfort, believing that was my purpose, to be a wealthy woman who gives away her wealth to help others.

But now I know that was a projection.

So what is my purpose?

My purpose is to collect stories wherever I am and whatever I'm doing.

This is my purest form of purpose.

Stories are my lifeline. They are how I connect with the world.

They move through me, touch the part of me that longs to help, and extend outward so others can be connected to them too.

I use these stories to shape the spaces I curate, the experiences I design, and the care I offer. Stories inform how I lead, how I follow, how I listen, and how I respond.

Collecting, sensing, and spending time with stories is how I honor my service to humanity.

Every part of what I do is informed by a story. I live for stories. To hear from others. To learn about them in every way.

I might add that my purpose is not about being a container for trauma or holding space for repeated pain. What is unique about my purpose is that I'm drawn to the change in the story. I listen for evolution. I get excited about movement. I thrive on the parts of stories when something shifts.

I am deeply interested in:

What happened?
What did you do?
How did you survive?
What shifted?

I'm gifted in many areas. As a leader, I'm highly skilled. I'm thoughtful. I consider people before myself when I'm working. My gifts don't define my purpose. They are an expression of it. They are what I do because I lead with purpose.

I am excellent at what I do, whether that's project management, helping an organization with AI adoption and readiness, or organizing an AI workshop, because I connect stories told, untold, and those I can foresee shaping.

Here's what I mean.

Years ago, I was a gate agent. I loved it. I didn't know why I loved it so much until recently. The act of serving as a gate agent allowed my purpose to guide how I delivered exceptional service. I can now look back and see how my purpose was affirmed by the number of awards, customer compliments, and feedback assessments I received.

As a gate agent, I was exceptional not only because I am an operational efficiency expert, but because I listened. I listened to customers share their travel stories all day. I instinctively learned patterns and themes as more data came in through human-to-human experiences. I used those stories to improve the customer experience.

Let me share a few examples.

In Minnesota, it's not uncommon to service an incoming crew and passengers by bringing a jet bridge to the plane when it's nine degrees below zero. When the jet bridge opens at the gate, freezing temperatures hit everyone. It truly is an unforgettable chill.

During those cold winter days, I noticed something. I saw passengers leaving the gate area or grabbing extra coats. I heard passengers talk about how cold it was as boarding began.

So I started preparing them.

I'd tell passengers seated in the gate area what was about to happen. I offered them the opportunity to move, use the restroom, or find another seat before boarding. For passengers beginning to board, especially those traveling with small children who needed to leave strollers at the end of the jet bridge, I reminded them how cold it would be and encouraged them to organize themselves as best as possible. I guided them to put jackets on small children in case there was a backup in the jet bridge.

These were small ways I could help. At the time, it wasn't clear to me why caring came so naturally. I was very good at the care part of my job. The stories shaped my actions.

Another way I served my purpose was by paying close attention to passengers who required additional assistance. For instance, if I noticed passengers with tight connections who needed wheelchair support, I made sure to provide them with extra care. This attention to detail ensured their transition between flights was as smooth and comfortable as possible.

I'd call the arriving gate ahead to ensure a wheelchair provider was waiting and let them know I was the gate agent for the passenger's next flight and that the connection was tight.

These small gestures were really about what I learned from the stories. The human moments that mattered to me and moved me to act.

When the passenger arrived, I'd greet them with, "I've been waiting for you. I'm so happy to see you."

And it was true.

A successful travel story that I could positively impact became my joy. My honor.

My purpose in collecting stories was to use what I was gifted with, and what was available to me, to improve someone's life experience.

My purpose is to collect stories. Stories are my oxygen.

My purpose hasn't always been clear to my mind, but it has always been clear to my heart.

I'm here to hear, to honor, and to respond with what I've. That thread has remained constant, even as my roles have changed.

When I was promoted from gate agent to performance manager, it wasn't the title that moved me. It was what I could do with the stories my employees told me.

Naming this is a profound declaration for me because it reshapes how I respond to every inquiry, every invitation, and every request for my time.

I no longer ask, What's in it for me?

Instead, I see each moment as an opportunity to collect stories. To be present not just to the person, but to the initiative, the energy, and the unfolding.

And when I offer something back, I do so in love and generosity, guided by what I can contribute without betraying my purpose.

That's a very different way of thinking.
A very different way of leading.

I no longer enter conversations looking to extract.

I'm out here polishing the stones I've gathered. Each story is a piece of a larger puzzle, or perhaps a clue, a truth waiting for the appointed time to be amplified so I can continue to serve humans.

I trust that when that time comes, I'll know precisely how each story fits into an organizational solution I suggest, a speaking engagement topic, an answer to a panel question, or a conversation about funding.

This is more than storytelling.

I'm polishing stories as stones to give away and share. I carry the stories to honor their dignity and to further advance humanity in ways we each can respect and thrive.

Parable of the Builder

There once was a woman who stood at the edge of an empty lot, laying bricks.
She was building.

As people arrived with new bricks, she graciously accepted them and continued her work.

The bricks were beautiful. Smooth. Strong. Varied in color. Some came from thousands of miles away. Some from mountain villages, others from coastal towns. No one knew why she collected them, only that each one seemed to arrive just when it was needed.

People grew curious.

"What are you building?" they asked.

She smiled but kept working. She thought, *I really don't know. They are here for a future time. I'm confident I'll know when the time comes.*

Soon came the advice.

"You should sell two bricks and keep one," said a merchant.
"You should build a fence and charge admission," said a strategist.
"You should livestream the process," said a marketer.
"You should scale," said the consultant.
"You should monetize," said the investor.

She listened, but her hands kept moving. Brick by brick, the structure rose.

She grew exhausted.

She had a vision for what to do with the bricks, and each time she tried to execute it, she felt unfulfilled. She grew tired of trying and tired of the noise.

Her vision was simple. A hub. A place where people could gather, pause, rest, and reconnect with their true leadership selves. She wanted others to collect their own stories.

She didn't know if it would scale.
She didn't know what the profit margins would be.

She only knew that the right materials always arrived, and her job was to lay them down.

Still, the scalers came.

"How will you grow?"
"How will you compete?"
"How will you win?"

She finally looked up and said,

"I am not building a business. I am following a call. I am here to collect and build."

And with that, she placed another brick.

* * *

Not every builder is chasing a million-dollar exit.

Some are answering a deeper call.
Some are laying foundations for futures unseen.

Some are taking the material they have and creating something the world doesn't yet know it needs.

Every builder deserves to protect the sanctity of their work.

In the age of AI, some builders are choosing purpose before code.

Let the builders build.

The Woman and the Scattered Stars

"I understand now that no one else in the world knows what I should do… Because no one has ever lived or will live this life I am attempting to live. Every life is an unprecedented experiment. This life is mine alone. So I've stopped asking people for directions to places they've never been."
— Glennon Doyle

As I release the love contained in these pages into the world, I hope that I've earned your trust in my leadership. Perhaps you have learned more about me than you hoped or not enough. What I've learned is that while a particular mission associated with your purpose can change, your purpose is constant. It's the thread that weaves your values together.

However, purpose can't be found by following someone else's path. Others' stories may feel similar and even hopeful, but purpose comes by listening to the quiet wisdom within. It reveals itself over time through our experiences.

This book was a spiritual release for me, but also a love letter to leadership. And so I leave you with this last parable, one that honors those who have felt unseen, who carry dreams others do not understand, and who choose to build spaces of possibility while still defining their purpose. May you trust the quiet knowing, make the invisible visible, and realize that you are light first before trying to become a light for others.

* * *

Once, in a quiet village nestled between hills and uncertainty, lived a woman with a dream sewn deep into her soul. It beat like an ever-present tapping she could not ignore, though no one around her seemed to hear it. She asked the elders, the scholars, and the guides, "What should I do?" They pointed her down paths carried by others. But each path ended in emptiness. She returned each time to herself, dust on her shoes, a weary spirit, and tears in her eyes.

At night, when the people were asleep, she would look up. The stars blinked above like understanding eyes. And sometimes one would fall low enough for her to touch. When she touched one, something inside her lit up. She felt alive. She felt seen. She felt remembered.

These stars didn't speak in words, yet they felt familiar. Each one taught her something. They taught her how to listen beyond language, how to build without blueprints, and how to trust the tug of her own spirit. She began to understand they were not just visitors. They were guides. The stars were home.

But her home wasn't where her feet were planted. Her home was everywhere the stars touched.

She carved out a space in her heart, a sacred place for the stars. The neighbors noticed a difference. "Why create space in your heart for something you can't yet see?" they asked. She smiled, knowing the stars longed to meet her people. Her people, though unaware, would begin to live more fully because she made space in her heart for the stars.

Years passed. There she stood, quiet and radiant. Then one day, the highest official in her land invited her to journey to three cities, where her feet could touch down and see more stars. She walked their streets, felt their pulse, and saw her own dream reflected in their skylines. In those cities, she saw what she was holding in her heart. She saw a physical place and a bridge to get people there.

She returned with clarity. Her next course of action was to build community and bridges so the stars and people could gather.

She wanted to make the invisible visible and help her village remember what it had forgotten. Wonder is not distant. It's in the stars each of us has the capacity to make room for.

The woman who once felt stuck became the architect of connection. She built bridges. She built for vision. And in doing so, she eventually became a star herself, a star others could remember, touch, and feel. A star to help them radiate a life uniquely their own.

Where the Clue Lives

"The soul is like a wild animal—tough, resilient, savvy, self-sufficient and yet exceedingly shy. If we want to see a wild animal, the last thing we should do is to go crashing through the woods, shouting for the creature to come out. But if we are willing to walk quietly into the woods and sit silently for an hour or two at the base of a tree, the creature we are waiting for may well emerge, and out of the corner of an eye we will catch a glimpse of the precious wildness we seek."
— Parker J. Palmer

There was a time when I believed that being seen would lead to being chosen. That if I showed up for enough events, panels, and gatherings, someone would notice. They would hear what I do, feel the energy I carry, and offer something in return, a financial contract or a collaboration.

But I've learned that not everything needs to or will turn into a financial opportunity. The belief that it would was rooted in a transactional approach to ambition. I was hoping that visibility would naturally convert into value. And while visibility has its place, it's absolutely not the same as alignment.

Part of my purpose when gathering stories is to be out in the world without restriction. To move freely, without needing to sell, pitch, or perform. In environments where I am present, curious, and open, I feel most like myself. I feel whole.

I used to think that the more available I was, the more likely I would land paid opportunities. Now I know my presence in those spaces was about polishing my purpose. It was a way to get myself ready and comfortable in my own being, much like the rocks by the river.

Each encounter, each event, and each conversation was like polishing a stone. I was learning about new services, new ideas, and new people. I was gathering insight, and I loved every bit of it. The opportunities I enjoyed most didn't come from the spotlight. They came from moments when I was simply sharing what I had learned or helping someone make sense of a new idea, a challenge, or a possibility.

Simple presence.

It might seem odd that at this point in the book, I am just now defining purpose. But even as I was writing, I wanted to be sure

I was describing my journey accurately. I didn't want to rush the language or misrepresent the pace of its unfolding. According to Webster's Dictionary, purpose is "the reason for which something is done or created." It's a powerful definition and one that is deeply personal.

It's not surprising that when I searched for "purpose" on LinkedIn, there were far fewer posts than for "artificial intelligence," and those I did find had much lower engagement.

Why might that be?

I suspect it's because thinking about purpose is not how most people consider choosing a career. It's not how they imagine feeding their families. And as AI continues to be a growing force, people are finding ways to leverage it to escape poverty, reinvent themselves, or find new relevance in a shifting economy.

And yet, some of us are deeply drawn to purpose. We are wired to ask deeper questions. To link the thing we can't help but do with the place where we can best be of service. It takes time to align our innate gifts with meaningful contribution. It takes time to discover them at all. When that natural connection happens, it's an incredible and liberating feeling to begin being from that place.

Purpose does not always announce itself. Sometimes it whispers. When I stopped trying to turn every moment into a transaction, I began to hear my purpose more clearly and understand how it wanted to show up.

For me, writing this book was never just a collection of thoughts and reflections. My writing has served as a clearing. It took time to arrive here, a place of true vulnerability. Years, in fact. I've walked through seasons of barriers, trappings, and quiet hoping. I am eternally grateful for every person I've ever met, because each of you has been part of the change. The constant change that has helped me make sense of my leadership journey, not just as a leader in AI, but as a woman called to a unique purpose.

Now that the clearing is done, I see a fork ahead.

One path calls me to stay in AI, to continue learning about what lies on the horizon and at the forefront of innovation. To help ensure large populations are not left behind or made invisible in the systems we build. It has been my path for several years, one of creating innovative frameworks and helping people, communities, policymakers, students, employees, and leaders make sense of their experiences with AI. It's a path of love.

The other path invites me to study us more and to help humans connect the threads of goodness between us. It would be a path of gathering stories that honor joy and build bridges, no matter where we are in the world. This too is a path of love.

Both are sacred. Both are needed.

I do not yet know which path I will choose, whether I will combine them, or which path will ultimately choose me. But I trust that as I spend more time with the stories, the decision will become clearer.

For now, I will listen.
For now, I will wonder.
For now, I will stay open to the clues.

Where in your life are you being invited to listen? To hear what might be calling you.

I hope that our paths cross. I would be honored to learn from you. I would love to know how you follow your own clues and how you gather meaning from experiences that matter.

How have you named the quiet truths that shape the way you live, the way you lead, and the way you love?

Until then, I remain curious.

Epilogue
The Unmoving Traveler

There was once a seeker who longed for purpose.

They packed their bags many times, moving from place to place, changing jobs, meeting new colleagues, looking for horizons that promised meaning.

Each new address felt like a fresh beginning, each new friend like a doorway to discovery.

Yet one morning, as the sun rose and painted the walls with its quiet, familiar gold, the seeker realized something that shook them: they had never moved at all.

Day had carried them into night, and night into day. Seasons had wrapped them in warmth and cold, and years had delivered lessons like gifts left at their doorstep.

Healing had arrived in the rhythm of seasons and time, community had gathered around them like a circle of curiosity, and growth had unfolded like a tree stretching its glory toward the sky.

But through it all, the seeker remained in the same place, always with themselves.

They realized that no matter how many roads they walked, no matter how many doors opened for them, they could not escape the one companion who had never left: their own soul.

And upon that realization, they understood. Purpose wasn't hidden in distant lands or in the exertion of endless movement. Purpose was the quiet art of listening to the voice of the unmoving traveler—the voice that had been with them all along.

From that day forward, the seeker began to measure life by the depth of their presence, the honesty of their reflection, and the tenderness with which they carried themselves.

For the greatest gift to self was never outward. It was the unmoving pilgrimage of purpose within.

"We spiral home again and again, until we realize the spaces vast enough for our essence were never out there. They were formed within, through the courageous act of self-awareness and self-acceptance."

— Dr. Elizabeth M. Adams

An Invitation

This book ends here.
But the practice does not.

If you are closing these pages feeling a familiar tension between responsibility and rest, between performance and purpose, between what your organization demands and what your inner compass knows, I want you to know this:
You are not alone in that space.

This book is not an AI leadership manual. It's a record of inquiry. I wrote it because I stepped out of momentum long enough to listen for what mattered most, and I am still listening.

Choosing purpose before code is an ongoing leadership practice, one that continues to unfold as artificial intelligence reshapes our work, our systems, and our lives.

I am most alive in spaces where dialogue is allowed to breathe: fireside conversations, moderated discussions, or intimate gatherings where listening matters as much as speaking. Spaces where we can talk about AI and leadership together, without scripts or certainty.

If you'd like to invite me into that kind of conversation, you can learn more about how I work at www.eadams.tech.

There is no formula here.
Only the possibility of facing this moment together.

ABOUT THE AUTHOR

Dr. Elizabeth M. Adams is an award-winning Responsible AI strategist, TEDx speaker, and recognized LinkedIn Top Voice whose work focuses on helping leaders and organizations navigate artificial intelligence without losing sight of what makes us human. With more than 30 years of technology leadership experience and as one of the few scholars globally to hold a doctorate in Leadership of Responsible AI, she brings a rare blend of academic rigor, global perspective, and modern AI relevance to the rapidly evolving technology landscape.

Dr. Adams is the founder of the Minnesota Responsible AI Institute, where she serves as Chief Engagement Officer, and founder of EMA Advisory. Across these roles, she brings a people-first lens to how leaders interpret and act on AI, advancing approaches that strengthen human judgment, workforce readiness, sustainability, and long-term economic resilience. Grounded in the belief that technology should expand human possibility, she is known for her steady, systems-level perspective and her ability to translate complex technology shifts into clear insights that support both innovation and human flourishing.

Her work bridges academia, industry, government, and civil society, returning to the same essential question: how do we ensure people thrive in the age of artificial intelligence?